HAWK SAFARI

The Search For a Rare Bird
A Curtiss Hawk P6-E

Ralph Rosanik

LION PUBLICATIONS
LINCOLN, NEBRASKA

ISBN 0-9637153-0-5

Lion Publications
10019 Bloomfield Dr. • Omaha, NE 68114
(402) 453-0369 • (402) 391-3450

Acknowledgments

*My Deepest Gratitude To All Those Who Helped Make
My Dream, The HAWK P6-E, A Reality*

Construction	*Wings*
Herb Tischler	Arnold Neiman

Fabric, Dope, Install Engine	*Engine Rebuild*
Larry Jensen & Wife	Steward-Davis
Dick Cooper	

Final Metal Work & Cosmetics, Paint, Assembly, Engine Functions
Terry Fritsch
Gene Stanley
Ralph Rosanik
Marvin Jenkins

Machine Work
Norman Savine & the many tool & die makers of
Central States Tool & Die Works
Production Tool & Die Works

Research, Development, Finance
Ralph Rosanik

The HAWK P6-E Support Crew
Crew Chief ....Terry Fritsh
Assistant Crew Chief...................................Gene Stanly
Administration & Public Relations ....Russ DeVoe
Stand-By Pilot...Gerry Strunk
Ground Crew ....Art Hill

Historians and Sources of Information Through the Years

Hank Leslie	Ken Wilson	Bob Cavanough
Don Knudsen	Jack Taft	Neil November
John Hauser	Bergan Hardesty	Gerry Abbamont
Bob Taylor	Hundreds of Others	

and
COLONEL PAUL JACOBS, Ret. US Army Air Corps
P6-E #32-256 Pilot, Engineering Officer At Selfridge Field
Beginning 1929 And During Existance Of Curtiss Hawk P6-Es

Special Thanks to George Schworm, Cynthia Almquist, and
Don Smithy, Manager of Omaha Epply Airfield

Photo courtesy of Prusha Photography, Omaha, NE

I dedicate this book to the memory of my wife

"Angie"

*I lost her to cancer one year before
completion of the Hawk P6-E*

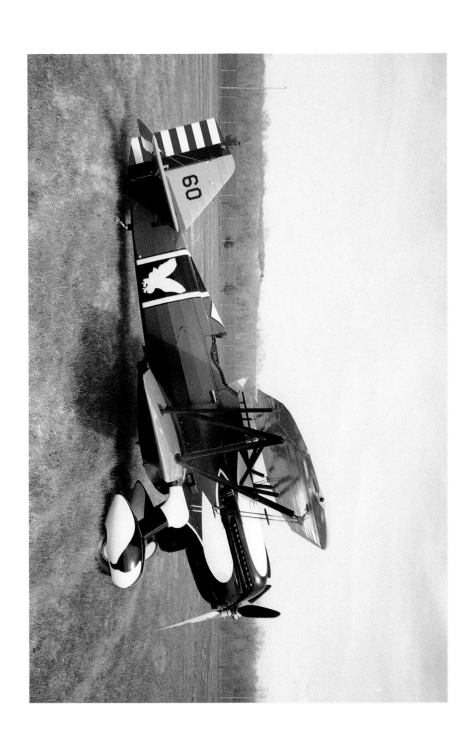

Contents

Foreword ix

1   The Origin of a Life of Continuous Adversity 1

2   A Plaster Lath Airplane 21

3   More of the Same 29

4   Sidetracked Again 47

5   The Rumor 69

6   Guatemala and the Captain 74

7   Lima, Peru and Emilio 86

8   La Paz, Bolivia 95

9   Flight to Cochobamba, Bolivia 102

10 Santa Cruz, Bolivia 108

11 Flight to Nowhere 109

12 Hostage 112

13 Initiating the Dream 114

14 Black Sunday 133

15 Embezzlement 137

16 More Turmoil 141

17 Shattered Dreams 145

18 Subterfuge and Deceit 152

19 The Ultimate Tragedy 154

20 In Limbo 156

21 Rebirth of a Hawk 158

22 More Ground Time 163

23 An Exercise in Futility 167

24 One for the Historians 174

Foreword

Delivery of the Curtiss Hawk P6-E5, last of the Army Air Corps open cockpit fighter biplanes, began in December of 1931. Only 46 were built—45 were eventually destroyed or scrapped. The only remaining example is on display at the Air Force Museum at Dayton, Ohio. It is non-flying, the engine inoperable, and more of a mock-up.

I became enchanted with this aircraft at a very early age. I thought it to be the most beautiful biplane and airplane ever built. I continued to feel that way into adulthood when it became an obsession. I decided to attempt to acquire one. This is my story of how it finally happened.

The Curtiss Hawk P6-E was the pivotal point of my entire life. My story tells of the hardship, adversities, subterfuge, greed and treachery that permeates a segmant of society and affected my lifetime effort to accomplish my dream.

There may be sections in this story—personal, business and other outrageous events—that seem to deviate from the actual intent. I felt they must be included to explain the continuing delays that occured over a period of 35 years that affected not only the development of the Hawk, but also my home life and my wife and family to the point of near personal self-distruction. The perpetual adverse events we had to endure to completion of the Hawk—and then, without my wife, Angie. I lost her to cancer one year before the airplane was finished. She had endured more than a husband should expect from a wife in tolerating and sacrificing so very much to participate in this never ending endeavor.

This story is true, covering my life from birth to the present day. From my pre-teen childhood—when aviation became an obsession—through the years when the Curtiss Hawk P6-E became my ultimate goal in spite of the unbelievable obstacles that developed throughout my entire life.

CHAPTER ONE

The Origin of a Life of Continuous Adversity

Born August 11, 1918, in Omaha, Nebraska, of immigrant parents, I wondered all my life what factors determined my destiny. A deserting father—leaving behind an almost fatally ill wife and a six month old son? Environment—a depraved social climate? I came to the conclusion that all the preceding, including my erroneous choice of friends and associates both in my own business and other ventures.

My mother was Italian, my father Austrian (that is all I know about him). My mother never discussed my father during the entire time of her life with me. I lost her to cancer while I was in the U.S. Army Air Corps during World War II. I was 24 years old.

I was born in a shabby tenement building in the worst section of Omaha. While my mother was giving birth to me, my father could not be found (later she learned he was in a saloon, drunk, as usual). I was delivered by a mid-wife at the tenement apartment.

Shortly thereafter, my mother became seriously ill during the influenza epidemic of 1918-1919 and almost died. It was during this illness that my father, with a woman, tried to kidnap me.

My mother had been moved to one of her sisters' homes because the cost of hospital care was out of the question. She was in the sub-basement of the building; her sister, my aunt, lived on the floor above.

My father, with the unknown woman, sneaked into the lower level of the building and into the bedroom where my mother lay. She was weak and semi-conscious, but cried out when my father grabbed me and ran for the door. My aunt upstairs heard mother's scream.

Now my Aunt was a typical little robust, stout Italian lady. She came rushing downstairs with a butcher knife in hand, grabbed my father, threatened him, seized me from his arms, and chased him out into the street—all the while shrieking appropriate expletives in Italian, descriptive of her thoughts of him at that moment. That is the last time he was seen or heard of; he just disappeared. Not once did he attempt to find out what kind of a son he had fathered.

This left an indelible scar on my mind. I did not miss him in the sense of missing him; I was outraged that he had left us in this horrible environment and grew to hate him. It is odd that we never once mentioned or discussed my father, nor did I ask.

During the first five years of my childhood, we continued to live in the tenement building we had returned to after my mother recovered from her illness. The building was a block long and two stories high. We lived in a one-room apartment on the lower level. There were no white people; all the tenants were blacks and Mexicans.

Across the street was a block-long one-story brick building that housed many prostitutes, both white and black. It was Omaha's red light district. As I recall, it was a pretty busy place, particularly weekends. Also, it was a danger zone for me. The ladies of ill-repute were constantly trying to entice me, a little five-year-old, into their dens—I think only to tease me.

At the end of the block on the same side of the street as the dens of denizen was an old-time saloon. When I ventured across the street, careful to skirt the danger zone, I would visit the saloon. Most of the customers knew me, called me Ralphie, gave me pennies (or if more charitable, maybe a nickel) then shoo me out.

Adjacent to the saloon was a junkyard operated by a Mr. Rothenberg. Now, in the saloon, on the floor along the foot-rail, were solid brass spittoons. Until I was stopped, I would occasionally sneak in, pick up a spittoon, go next door, and sell it to Mr. Rothenberg for an unreasonably small sum. As a result, I started calling him Mr. *Rottenberg*. Strangely enough, the saloon owner must have had a large supply of spittoons because they seemed to be replaced immediately. I can only guess, at this late date, that Mr. Rottenberg sold them back to him. In my case, if something was not nailed down, look out. With me, even at the age of five, it was bare survival.

The few playmates I had were mostly Mexican and a few blacks. When you grow up in this environment, you don't think about race, color, or other prejudices. In the apartment next to ours (if we dare to call them apartments), lived an elderly black gentleman, Mr. Nash, who adopted me as his friend. He took me fishing with him often. My mother was away, working to eek out a living as a house cleaner in private homes and a few small hotels. Mr. Nash was a wonderful cook and made the best pancakes I have ever eaten in my life.

Of course, my mother and I had no social life of any kind. It was just working day and night for her. She was uneducated and could not read or write. When I started school I would bring my school books home; as I studied my lessons, I would include her, and together we learned to read. I also taught her to write. She got to the point where she could read the newspaper and basic word books—not easily, but she did it. She was a wonderful, beautiful lady with a heart of gold, and patient beyond reason.

Among the very few playmates I had through grade school were two Mexican boys my age. Their names were Ramon and Simon Noriega. Their mother and father took me in as part of the family. As a result, I learned to speak pretty good Spanish and to this day enjoy the Mexican diet as much as the Italian.

When it came time to register me in grade school—in my case, I was 6 years old because I was stricken with a severe case of scarlet fever while I was five and had almost died—my mother took me to a school, but since she could not speak English, her pronunciation of our last name was unclear to the person taking the registration information. As a result, the interpretation of my name came out as "Rosnick," not "Rosanik" as it should have been. For most of my life, I had no way of knowing this—until I was invited to dinner with a friend. A Catholic Priest from Chicago was visiting Omaha and came to dinner with us. When we were introduced, he remarked that he knew a Jewish family in Chicago by my name, "Rosnick", knew them well and by chance was I related to them. I was puzzled and answered that I had no relatives in Chicago, was not Jewish, was Catholic, and am Italian.

As time passed, I continued to wonder about my name. I finally went to the courthouse to check my mother and father's marriage certificate. I then learned the correct spelling and pronunciation of my name. It is pronounced "Row-sah-nik," spelled, "Rosanik." I only clear this up because so many people do not know what to call me.

About the time I started grade school, the tenement building we lived in was condemned and we had to move. A few blocks away was a small house in an industrial and warehouse district across the street from a large icehouse that produced most of the ice for the Omaha area.

By now I was starting to be income productive at the age of six. The icehouse was a good source of product for me to merchandise. I became friendly with the men working there and developed a business relationship with them whereby they would provide me with surplus blocks of ice of various sizes. Sometimes, large blocks of ice were on the shipping dock to be picked up for delivery. I could only assume that some of these were for me, and since no one was around, I would load my orange crate wagon, take off, and sell the ice blocks for whatever was reasonable. To be competitive with the ice company, I of course, gave substantial discounts to my customers and developed a route that was predominantly low income clients, poor people, and sold them blocks or chunks of ice for a fraction of what the ice company did. In those days, everyone had iceboxes, not refrigerators as we know them today.

When summer and warm weather passed, I had to find other sources of income. I sold newspapers, delivered circulars for printing companies, delivered Western Union messages, delivered groceries for a few of the small grocery stores, and built a stockpile of coal for winter sales.

My coal enterprise was the most harrowing of all my business ventures. My source of inventory was the railroad tracks at the east end of Omaha. I would drag my orange crate wagon a mile or so away from where we lived. There would be rows of coal cars lined up for blocks and blocks—what an inventory! The coal cars were open top and loaded to the brim, so much so that when the train moved, large amounts would fall to the ground and could be picked up by anyone. This was easier than the ice business. It was light work to pick up small pieces of coal, load them in the wagon, go off and sell to my summer clients, return, reload, and continue my route.

On one occasion, this profitable venture was almost terminated because of a misunderstanding on my part. On a particular trip to replenish my stock for future sales, there was a shortage of fallen coal on the ground. As with the ice business—when I provided myself with blocks of ice from the dock when no one was around—I took for granted that there was no problem if I climbed atop the coal cars and collected coal from the inside.

I was inside the coal car, below the side panel top, not deliberately trying to avoid being seen from the ground, when a loud banging echoed through the steel side panel of the car. Along with the banging, someone was shouting: "What the hell are you doing in there?" I hesitated, raised my head above the edge of the coal car, trying to think of a quick story.

"Get out of there!" he screamed. He was a railroad security agent I had seen many times, but always steered clear of to avoid any confrontation with him or to give him the opportunity to recognize me because of my very frequent visits.

He was standing next to my partially full wagon as I climbed out of the car. He grabbed me by the collar, threatened to have me arrested and thrown in jail. I told him there was not enough coal on the ground, and I needed some to take home to heat our house. We had no furnace, just a coal stove both for heating and cooking. He growled, mumbled something, reminded me to take only chunks of coal on the ground. The next time I went after coal, I took a lookout with me, one of my Mexican friends.

Once again we had to move. The little two-room house we had lived in for the past one and a half years was to be torn down. By now I was between six and seven years old. We moved into a two-story brick building and occupied the upper three-room apartment.

We were still in the same area because of the low rental costs. Unfortunately, my mother did not know that we were back in the same type of area where I was born. There were no homes, just railroad warehouses, truck garages and a small hotel two blocks away that housed railroad laborers.

The most disagreeable aspect of the area was another block-long row of houses of prostitution. This turned out to be another unpleasant experience for me. Once again, the ladies would taunt me, chase me down the street—and one time one caught me, but I broke away from her. I was seven years old and terrified. I ran home, crawled under a porch, and cried my heart out. This happened two times during our stay at that location. I never told my mother or anyone for years.

It was at this location that I became, I am sure, the youngest bootlegger, if not in the world, at least in Omaha. I had learned of a place on the south side of town where I could buy homemade alcohol. I was eight years old by now and constantly seeking new business ventures.

I would board a streetcar to the other side of town, seek out the supplier, purchase a gallon of 190-proof alcohol, re-board a streetcar, and head for my laboratory—a large wooden box I had converted into a shed. I would gather empty whiskey bottles from the river bottom and all the places I knew where the hoboes and alcoholics hung out. After all, I knew most of them.

After returning to my laboratory, I would wash the bottles with my usual sanitary system. Then I would dilute the 190-proof alcohol with three gallons of water, reducing it to approximately 60-proof, fill my pint bottles, and chart my delivery route and schedule. I had no trouble marketing my product. My clients welcomed me with open arms. After all, they did not have to leave their habitats in the river bottom and jungles. The small hotel nearby, where many railroad laborers lived, was my best and most profitable source. They were heavy drinkers, and my schedule coincided with their paydays.

The most frightening experience I had was when transporting a gallon of alcohol in a glass jug. I was alighting from the streetcar I had taken from South Omaha to North Omaha. The streetcar had three cast steel steps. I was carrying the gallon jug in a paper shopping bag. As I stepped down, the jug struck the steps and shattered to pieces, the alcohol pouring over the steps and street below. As the conductor stood up to see what had happened, I dropped what was left and ran as fast as I could, my investment literally down the drain.

Another means of generating income was what we called "Junking" back in those days of the late twenties and early thirties. I would get my trusty orange crate wagon and go forth all over town, picking up scraps of steel, aluminum, electric wiring, copper, brass, tin—anything that may or may not have been nailed down I could sell to Mr. Rottenberg. Walking along the railroad tracks was a good way to find scrap iron. I always took my crowbar with me in case I found any superfluous items of steel such as spikes only halfway into ties, rail plates coming loose, and of course, even miscellaneous pieces actually laying on the ground.

When my wagon was loaded, I would journey to my favorite junk man, Mr. Rottenberg. We got to know each other very well, and our meetings always turned into heavy discussions concerning what I expected to be paid and what he intended to pay. We seldom agreed; however, I came up with a method of equalizing our negotiations, initially, I think, unbeknown to him.

When we settled on any transaction, if I felt shorted, I said nothing since I had a plan in mind which I felt justified in exercising. I would leave on good terms and wait for the weekend. The junkyard was closed during that time. I went around to the alley, climbed over the fence, retrieved my junk, waited until Monday, and resold it to him at a handsome profit.

It seemed that I was too frequently interrogated by the police. Many times I would walk past the police station, which was not too far from where I lived, with my burlap sack full of copper and brass wiring scrap swung over my shoulder. By then I was eight years old, strong enough to carry loads on my back. Many of the policeman and detectives knew me, but often took me into the station, opened my sack to inspect the contents, and reminded me that anything I had in the sack could only come from scrap piles as discarded materials. Echoes of the railroad detective.

Fruit and vegetables were a rarity in our household, something a person does not give much thought to. We survived on very basic items of food. My mother was a wonderful cook. She made our own pasta, rolled the dough and sliced it into strips. Baked wonderful homemade Italian bread. Soups. Ravioli. Chicken was our main food. Seldom did we have meat. It was my duty to supply fruits and vegetables. Under a bridge over the Missouri river at the east end of Omaha was a cannery. Outside were parked open-top railroad cars similar to coal cars. There were chutes protruding from openings in the side of the cannery building. Fruits and vegetables unsuited for canning were discharged into the chutes and out to the rail cars to be hauled to a disposal location.

I would take a market basket, go to the cannery, climb into the rail cars, sort through the contents, and pick out the best items of fruits and vegetables. Surprisingly enough, I would come home with a very good supply of produce.

**My mother Rose Marie (left) and her sister Rosario.
At the turn of the century.**

A Sunday afternoon at Omaha airport, mid-1930s.

I flew passengers in the front Stinson Reliant at age 16.

The boys and I at Omaha airport, early 1930s (next three pages). I'm on the left in the first photo, third from the left in the second photo, and on the left in the third photo.

The United Airlines Boeing Roscoe Turner wanted to look at, mid-1930s.

Hanford Airliner I serviced at age 16.

Enzminger and Son, my first airport job, early 1930s.

I soloed in this plane, a J6-5 Travelair.

Me going out to fly, 1933, in an OX-5 Travelair.

This was the weather plane I flew before it crashed (next page) in the early 1930s.

The Pilot, Jim Goggins, was not injured.

Council Bluffs, IA, Airport, early 1930s. I flew all of these.

One-eyed, peg-legged, Wolf Powell and his airplane, which I flew a lot. Early 1930s.

**Amelia Earhart checks her maps during a stop in Omaha in September 1935 . . .
With her are stunt pilot Paul Mantz, left, and her husband, George Palmer
Putnam. This is the day I serviced her airplane.**

Photo courtesy of Omaha World-Herald

CHAPTER TWO
A Plaster Lath Airplane

The next two years, up to the age of ten, I continued finding ways to produce income while going to school. About that period I began to notice airplanes flying overhead. My interest grew, and I began to dream of flying and airplanes constantly. An impossible dream. How could someone like me, from the ghetto, questionable future, ever have the opportunity to realize such a dream?

Between school and my work schedule, I had little spare time, but I began to build model airplanes in what time I did have left. After I had built a few, I decided, why not build a full-size, *real* airplane?

I gathered all the wooden boards and plaster laths I could find or obtain somehow, got hammer, nails, and saw, and began construction of an airplane comparable to the size of a Cub. The fuselage was square, wings were square, tail assembly square and angled to shape, landing gear out of two-by-fours with coaster wagon wheels I had obtained from Mr. Rottenberg's junk yard at the usual convenient time.

I had built the plane in a small yard in front of where we lived, and although there was little regular traffic because of the area, trucks and horse wagons passing by would stop, and people would come over and talk to me as I sat in the cockpit; they seemed to get quite a kick out of it. I would sit in it, pretend it was real. Whenever I heard the roar of an airplane overhead, I would look up, close my eyes, and pretend it was me up there.

Building the airplane inflamed my dream and wish for the real thing. I tried to quench my passion for airplanes and flying by reading all the books and magazines I could afford, and I went to the library often. It wasn't enough.

By now I was between eleven and twelve years old. I was very mature. I had not had a normal childhood. I was almost full grown and looked and acted much older than my age. What could I do about this burning desire to be near airplanes, to fly?

There was a solution. I boldly went to the airport to see if I could get a job—doing anything. The job must provide me first with income, and second with a chance to learn how to fly, somehow at no cost to me since I had to give my wages to my mother to help in our survival.

There were only two flying services, Enzminger Aircaft and Burnam & Miller Flying Service, in Omaha at that time. I went first to Enzminger, told him I wanted to work around airplanes *and* learn to fly.

He looked at me in a strange, quizzical kind way with a smiling glint in his eyes, asked how old I was, and a few more questions. He said he would give me a steady job if I could handle the hours and means of getting to the airport after school and on weekends. I assured him this was not a problem.

Well, it was somewhat of a problem; it was ten miles to the airport. In the beginning, I walked the distance after school and on weekends. Then I had an idea. If I could acquire a bicycle, it would solve my transportation needs. But how and where would I get a bicycle? To me, in my situation, not having the money to buy one, the answer was simple, a visit to my source of equipment, my private warehouse: Mr. Rottenberg's stock pile. Unfortunately (or fortunately), he was closed on the weekend. I needed the parts as soon as possible so I found it necessary to use my usual procedure. I found enough pieces and parts to build a bare frame bicycle, less tires. That, however, was not a problem; I had other sources for them.

I was overjoyed with my new job. It did not seem possible that I had achieved my first step. A kid from the bottomlands of the city, a borderline urchin, questionable business methods and ethics, could elevate himself into this wonderful world in the sky.

My duties were to gas airplanes, clean and sweep the hangar, wash company airplanes, help the mechanics, and on Sundays, sell airplane rides. Exciting experiences were the many barnstorming trips I got to go on on weekends. It was my job to keep the airplanes gassed, sell rides after we landed in meadows or cornfields near small towns.

Whenever transient aircraft stopped in Omaha for fuel or service, I would run out into the field to wave them in to get their gas business. The other flying service also had a line boy who did the same thing. The competition was fierce. The times were of the recession of the thirties. There were perpetual verbal battles between the owners and employees of both companies. Everyone called everybody across the way "Longtailed rats." And they meant it.

Some of the most cherished and memorable experiences I had as a line boy were meeting and talking to many of the aviation legends who stopped in Omaha for service. Among them were Amelia Earhart,

Rosco Turner, Jimmie Doolittle, many of the race pilots, movie stars of the period, Wallace Beery, Tom Mix, and many more. The one person who has always stayed in my mind above all the others was Amelia Earhart. She was so sweet and kind to this young boy who broke his neck to service her airplane—the red Lockheed Vega she flew on many of her record-breaking flights and journeys.

And Roscoe Turner—How could one ever forget him? When he came through Omaha (I cannot recall what make of airplane he was flying), I waved him in for service. He instructed me of his needs, and as we stood talking, he saw a Boeing 80-A parked in front of United Airlines service hangar and said he wanted to go look at it. As he walked away, I thought in wonderment: Now This Is The Ultimate Aviator. He was dressed in the picturesque outfit he was so well known for, the tan twill banjoed jodhpurs, mirror-finished leggons and shoes, the military jacket with polished Sam Brown Belt (I wondered where the saber was) tan shirt and black tie, the jauntily cocked officers cap—and that waxed tapered-to-a-needlepoint mustache, turned up at the ends. If only I'd had a camera—better yet, a movie camera—to catch that swaggering walk. Incidently, we had an Italian pilot of sorts in Omaha who tried to imitate Roscoe Turner's attire. Dressed in an outfit almost identical to Roscoe's outfit, he would go all over town, proclaiming himself a "Pilot." When he did fly, however, most of his landings were of the crash-landing variety. What a character.

Now that I had wriggled my way into aviation through the slot at the bottom of the door, my next step and challenge was: how would I learn to fly? My meager wages were for bare survival. I gave my earnings to my mother, keeping only a few nickels to buy a candy bar or soda pop occasionally. And all of my time was devoted to company work.

I proposed an arrangement to my employer that would allow me some free time. If I completed all my tasks and took care of line service, could I be allowed to work for other airplane owners? He looked at me with that strange quizzical look, with the glint in his eyes, smiled, and said we could try it and see if it would work.

I am not sure I knew what a whirling dervish was, but if it is something that whirls and swirls at high speed, then that is what I turned into. I was now fourteen, looking like sixteen. One must be sixteen years old to get a student permit to fly. I worked out an arrangement with owners that every time I washed their airplane, I would get ten minutes of flying time. I took care of several different makes of airplanes, and in the next year (by the time I was fifteen) accumulated enough time to start taking lessons.

With all my riding with the many pilots in the many different airplanes, and they letting me handle the controls, I was well prepared to start taking lessons. Everyone knew I was not sixteen and could not get a student permit, but they started giving me lessons anyway.

I had built up twelve hours of flying time over a period of almost two years in twelve different makes of planes with twelve different flying characteristics. I would take fifteen minutes of instruction in one type of plane one day and a few days later take ten or fifteen minutes of time in another type. The planes I flew were OX-5, J6-5, J-5, J6-9 (cabin), Gipsey, all Travelairs. OX-5, J6-5, F-2, Wacos. OX-5 and J6-5 Robins, SM-8A, and Junior Stinson, all before I soloed in a J-5 Travelair. These were planes I took instruction in. I rode in many, many more different makes.

My periods of instruction were erratic because the plane owners were not always around when I was free to fly. The time before my solo flight was spread over a long period, between the ages of fifteen and sixteen, because I was not supposed to solo until I was sixteen. However, when no one was around . . .

One day, when I was warming up an OX-5 Travelair biplane to take some instructions, I was in the rear cockpit and saw the Civil Aeronautics Agency inspector coming my way. He knew I was under age. As he approached, I shrunk below the cockpit rim to hide. The owner of the plane, a one-eyed, peg-legged pilot named Wolf Powel, was standing beside the cockpit and turned toward the inspector, trying to shield me. The inspector, a large handsome man—his name was Monté—asked who was in the cockpit since it was obvious the engine was not managing itself.

Wolf answered that he had a student to give instruction to, and Ralphie—as everybody called me—was just warming up the engine. Monté came to the side of the cockpit and tapped me on the head. I raised my head above the rim and stared wide-eyed at Monté. I had no physical certificate or student permit because of my age and thought this was the end of my flying career forever. Monté gave me a stern look, again tapped me on the top of the head, broke into a grin, and warned me to be careful and not let him catch me again until I was sixteen. After he was safely gone, I taxied out and went flying.

I will never forget my first instruction flight with Wolf Powell in his

OX-5 Travelair. I was in the rear cockpit, he in the front. We flew off the turf in those days; many of the planes had tail skids. Although I had flown ships in the air when riding with many of the fellows, this was different. I managed to take off decently and continued straight ahead, kept going straight ahead on and on. I did not know Wolf was planning to have me try a landing on my first flight. He pulled the throttle and yelled,"Where are you going, on a cross-country? Go back and land." I got a little frustrated and kept going straight ahead till he jerked the stick into a left turn and shouted: "Hey, Hardnose, go back to the field and land." As a result, I came to be known around the field as Hardnose. And Wolf told everybody about my extended cross-country take-off leg.

A few months later, I reached sixteen, ready for my (second) first solo flight. That I accomplished on August 11, 1934, my sixteenth birthday. I had many hours coming from the previous years I washed airplanes and quickly built up my time and got my Private License.

Now that I had my License, I could carry passengers. I had flown practically every type of airplane on the field, and the owners allowed me to carry passengers on sight-seeing flights over town. I was just over sixteen. Many times I would sell tickets for airplane rides, escort the passengers to the beautiful Stinson Reliant five place ship, help them in, and show them how to buckle up. No one would be in the pilot's seat. The passengers would settle in and wait for the dashing macho pilot to appear to take them on the new exciting experience into the wild blue yonder.

When I was sure everyone was ready, I would climb into the pilot's seat in my work coveralls and start the engine. I suppose they thought I was just the mechanic warming up the engine for the chief pilot. After making sure everything was OK, I would begin to taxi out to the field. The passengers never seemed much at ease. Here was this young, skinny, baby-faced kid sitting at the controls of this big airplane with their lives in his hands. The owners of the airplanes would stand by and gleefully watch the passengers' reaction when I climbed into the pilot's seat.

As I had mentioned previously, these were the thirties, the depression years. Aviation was in its infancy. Other than a few jobs flying for airlines and a few businesses, it was difficult to make a living in aviation.

Now that I was sixteen years old, I managed to get a part time job with Hanford Airlines (they later became Continental Airlines) as a one-man ground crew. I would work four hours a day after school (from

6:00 P.M. to 10:00 P.M.) seven days a week servicing the Lockheed Air-liners, gassing them, loading and unloading baggage and mail. I guess I felt pretty important because I was required to wear a bullet belt with a western-type holster and .38 pistol. I was only sixteen.

From 3:30 P.M. to 6:00 P.M., I would work for both the flying ser-vices, alternately. When I was finished with the airline job every night at 10:00, I had another very interesting job: preparing a J6-9 Pitcarian weather plane for the midnight flight. This aircraft had instruments attached to the wing struts to check barometric pressures, temperatures, and other information needed to determine weather conditions daily. It was my duty to gas, oil, and preflight the plane every night. During winter, I had to warm the engine with heaters to facilitate quick starts in the frigid air. The flights were always scheduled for midnight. Unfortu-nately, this job ended abruptly when the plane crashed one morning and was completely destroyed. The pilot, Jimmy Goggins, survived. He was talked down in virtually zero-visibility conditions. He made an amazing crash landing. Before the crash, along with being paid for taking care of the Pitcarian, I also got to fly it.

While I was in high school, I continued to work at all these jobs. High school, I guess, was supposed to be a memorable experience. I can't say that in my case. My total existence was committed to aviation, so I had no time for school sports or other activities. And unpleasant sit-uations developed that not only caused me to withdraw from activities, but also from my classmates.

My mother and I continued to live in the disagreeable section of town all during my time in high school and for a few years after I gradu-ated. During my first year, it was natural for a few of the classmates, boys, to want to socialize. Because of my environment, I isolated myself and became virtually anti-social.

One Saturday night, about 9:00 P.M., I happened to be home, fortu-nately, otherwise my mother would have been exposed to what hap-pened. There was a loud banging on the front door, and the voices of several drunken young boys, my classmates, insisting on being invited in. Since the building we lived in was near the red light district, the boys assumed this was part of it and were looking for prostitutes.

I went to the door, started to open it slightly, saw who they were; I knew them and slammed the door before they recognized me. They con-tinued to bang on the door, cursing and screaming obscenities. Finally, they left. The next day I quit high school.

When I went to work that afternoon, the fellows at the airport asked why I was not in school. I told them I felt it was a waste of time. They encouraged me to return, which I did—until another incident happened.

I was taking Machine Shop and Auto Mechanics. The instructors were two brothers, each teaching one of the classes. The one who taught auto mechanics was an unpleasant person with an acid personality. Since I worked late every night, I had little rest and many times came to school tired and did not always function efficiently. The teacher knew how much I worked, but of course I knew that was no excuse as far as he was concerned. He came to ride me pretty heavily, and although I was an "A" student in all my classes and did my work in Auto Mechanics well, he made it a point to lower my grades to prevent me from being on the honor roll.

He did this three semesters in a row, so I decided to complain to the principal. He talked to the instructor, but this only angered the man. He then did an unforgivable act. I was working on a car and had ordered new brake shoes for it from the teacher. He gave them to me, and, before class was over, I had laid them by the wheels I was working on. The next morning, they were gone; I reported them missing. The teacher immediately accused me of stealing them and turned me over to the principal, who expelled me from school.

I later returned to the principal and insisted that I had not stolen the brake shoes, but he would only consider letting me back in school if I returned them or paid for them. He just would not believe me. I went back to the teacher and tried to convince him that I had not stolen them. He insisted that he knew I had; however, he seemed uncomfortable with my presence.

I became suspicious. Later that day, after I knew he had gone, I returned to his office, searched his desk, and unbelievably, found the brake shoes in one of the drawers. I took them to the principal and told him where I had found them. He seemed puzzled and uncertain what to do about the situation, but he did say I could return to school. I told him I did not think I would. I thought about it for three weeks and decided to return only to graduate and get a diploma. I knew I would need it for future verification that I did finish high school.

From then on, high school was unimportant. I isolated myself completely from everyone, only stayed long enough to graduate, another unpleasant experience.

Although I had all these jobs, the total income was meager. I worked at them to be near everything related to aviation and flying. Basic things like shoes and clothing were skimpy in our household. Throughout grade school and high school, my source of clothing was the Salvation Army shops. Up to the time I was ten years old, I seldom wore shoes; they were for special occasions, holidays. My young friends, the Mexicans, and I ran around barefoot all the time. For graduation from high school I had no suit to wear. I went to the Salvation Army store, found a suit too small for me. My mother was an excellent seamstress. She took three inches of folded material from the inside of the suit coat and sewed it to the bottom edge. The pants waist was too small, so she cut out a wedge of material and sewed it in the back. When I had the coat on, you could not see it. Well, since then, for many years, I have been considered one of the best dressed men in Omaha, not from an ego standpoint, but I suppose to mask a horrible inferiority complex I had developed.

CHAPTER THREE

More of the Same

During the Twenties, the U.S. Government was releasing contracts to aerial photograph the entire United States. The photos would be assembled into mosaic maps. This was one of the few lucrative operations available to private flying companies.

One of these companies hangared with the flying service I worked for, and I took care of their airplanes. I became friendly with the pilots and photographers, and in the course of conversations, I learned that there was a demand for aerial photographers. There were no schools that offered instruction in this type of photography. The only place to learn was the Army Air Corps Tech School. I was encouraged to join the Air Corps, and once I had learned the profession, the company would buy me out—during peace-time one could buy one's way out of the service for $120—and employ me immediately. The wages were good for the times, and I could do doubly well by alternating as pilot and photographer.

I had graduated from high school in March of 1937, and the diploma I stayed to get was necessary to join the Air Corps, which I did in December of 1937. I was sent to Chanute Field near Rantoul, Illinois, attended the Air Corps Tech School, and completed the ground and aerial photography course.

A notable, and amazing, thing happened during my first term in the Air Corps. After completing basic training at Chanute Field, we were to be transferred to Lowery Field in Denver, Colorado, to complete our aerial work. We would be the first class to open the Tech school of photography at Lowery Field.

There were thirty of us, and we were to be divided into three groups and flown to Denver in three Douglas B-18 bombers. I was to be in the second bomber to leave. The first one had left, and my group was being prepared and equipped with parachutes to board. But Mother Nature was calling for some latrine activity, and I was late to board the second flight. Another student took my place; I never knew who it was.

I boarded the third bomber with the last group and headed for Denver. When we arrived, we were told the most shocking news one could ever hear, particularly me. The second bomber had crashed, killing everyone on board. I later received a set of photographs of the wreckage. The airplane had been totally demolished, and there were parts scattered all around the countryside. One tries to evaluate something like this. Why was I spared? With all the adversity in my life up to this time, did I dare hope this could be the turning point? It wasn't. But I did live to fulfill my dream of the Curtiss Hawk P6-E which I already had in mind. At one time I remarked that I had never seen a P6-E. I did see one at Chanute Field in 1938 and took a picture of it. And this was more fuel to a dream that was developing.

By early 1939, I had completed the photography course and was ready to come home to a wonderful job in the sky. Had I known what was in store for me, I would have stayed in the Air Corps with the possibility of becoming a flying Cadet. War clouds were beginning to gather. All aerial mapping and photography contracts were being canceled. This meant no job awaiting me in Omaha. The photo outfit had shut down operations and informed me they would not be buying me out of the service.

During the pre-war days in the Air Corps, we were paid $21 a month. I sent this home to my mother. To supplement my income, I started a loan operation early in my enlistment that was pretty profitable. I never went anywhere and saved my money, so when the boys would run out of funds by the middle of the month, they would borrow from me at my rate of two to one. This generated good income, so I was able to send my mother more than just the $21 per month. Also, in case of an emergency, I would have funds. That is how I bought my way out of the service.

I hitchhiked home from Gardner Field in early 1939. It was not easy getting rides on the highway back then. Men in uniform were not too well treated or respected. People would assume the reason you were in the service was because you were unable to do anything else or you were just a plain goldbrick. It took four days to get to Omaha from California.

I managed to get many short hauls. I got to Wyoming, late at night, about 10:00 P.M. A car stopped and offered me a ride. It was dark, and all I could hear was a man's voice. I told him I was going to Omaha. Fortunately for me, he was going to Chicago and would go right through Omaha. I got in, and it was a black man, very friendly, wanted to know if I had eaten. I hadn't, so he said he would stop along the road and get some food since he had been driving all day, had not eaten either.

He stopped in front of a small café on the highway but hesitated to go in. In those days blacks were not received too well in white restaurants. He asked me to go in with him. The few people there stared at us, him black, me a low down soldier. They were not courteous at all, but did give us some sandwiches. I tell this so people can understand the social climate back then. Blacks still have a problem, but soldiers are now respected.

As we drove into the night, I felt the fellow was disturbed at the treatment and attitude of the people back at that restaurant. About 2:00 A.M., he said he was going to stop at the next store we came to and get a package of cigarettes. Stores and gas stations were few and far between along the highways back in 1939. We finally came to one. He stopped and said he would be only a few minutes. He then reached across me to the glove compartment, opened it, and took out a pistol.

Oh boy, what now? I thought.

He was gone about five minutes, came running out of the store, jumped into the car, and took off in a streak. There had been no gunshots, but I had an idea what happened. He'd remarked earlier that he did not have much money, so I had offered to pay for some of the gas with what little money I had. I was uneasy for the next day and a half, but he acted OK and drove me right up to my home in Omaha.

After returning home I stayed with my mother a few days, then headed for the airport, hoping to find something I could do there that would provide me a livable wage and still, as before, be in aviation.

It was good to see all the boys at the airport, and of course old Wolf had to address me as Hardnose. In fact, until he died a few years ago, when he would see me, he would get a crooked grin on his face, cock his one good eye, and still call me Hardnose—after almost forty-five years—and then stump off on his peg leg. But he was one hell of a pilot, taught hundreds of Cadets during World War II. When he passed away, his son knew of our relationship and gave me all his log books and his original pilot's license.

After checking everywhere at the airport, I found nothing available. So I met with several of the fellows; they all owned airplanes, but not for business. All of them had jobs as machinists, accountants, electricians, other trades, and flying was just a hobby—but they gave flying instruction and rides to support their hobby.

I asked them what I should do. They replied with the most classic statement I have ever heard in my life: "Look, Kid, get out of aviation. There's no future in it." Believe it or not, the next unbelievable thing I did was take their advice.

Since I had taken machine shop in high school, I went to work in a factory, initially, running a metal stamping punch press and doing other production work. It paid better than anything else I could find at the time. Very soon after I started, the company hired a German tool and die maker, put in a tool and die department, and moved me to the shop as a tool and die apprentice under the German toolmaker. This was 1940.

With my background, I learned quickly and worked at the trade for the next two years—until December 7, 1941. I assumed I would be drafted because of my previous service, so I decided to enlist back in the Air Corps with a chance of becoming a Flying Cadet rather than be drafted into some other branch of the service. This was a very difficult decision because I had to provide for my mother's subsistence. After all these years I had finally been able to provide her with a nice home in a respectable neighborhood, and this just since I got out of the Air Corps in early 1939.

When I went to enlist, and they found out that I was becoming a tool and die maker and also had the responsibility to care for my mother, I was deferred. Additionally, my trade was in the number one skilled labor priority category.

By December, 1943, the war was still raging, and I wanted to get into Cadets before it was all over. By now we were pretty well settled in our home. My mother knew my passion for flying. We discussed my joining the Air Corps once again, planned how to maintain her subsistence, and I enlisted in the service once more, specifically hoping to qualify for flying Cadet.

From Omaha, I was sent to Amarillo, Texas, for basic training and evaluation. We were told that we were the last group to be considered for Cadet training. There were 4,500 applicants in this group. Apparently, the tests were stiffer than usual, so we were told, with the result that there were wholesale washouts. Only 350 made it through; fortunately I was one of them.

Amarillo, Texas—boy!—the one place in the country you stand in water up to your knees and have dust blow in your face. I had a few humorous experiences when on bivouac during basic training. The first night we camped out in our pup tents. There were four of us in the tent.

During the night when I felt something moving, I thought it was one of the other fellows. When we got up at daybreak, something was still moving. We got a flashlight to see in the dim light. We all gave out a big scream and ran out of the tent—we had been sleeping on a nest of snakes! Another evening, just before dark, old Mother Nature was calling me for latrine activity. I found the designated ditch, a foot wide slot dug in the ground, and as I straddled it, slipped and fell in. Well, you can guess my condition. Now I know where that old saying came from: "You're full of * * * * up to your eyebrows."

While on basic training, we had to go on the usual 25 mile hike. There were three squadrons of about 64 men per squadron. I was in the middle group. We had our full back-packs, rifles, ammunition, and one canteen of water each to last the 25 miles. It was boiling hot, and as we progressed, men were dropping off like flies. The meat wagon (ambulance) was following behind, picking up the casualties. I was in the middle of the second flight and began dropping behind after about 15 miles. At 20 miles, I was trailing, all by myself, a half mile behind of what was left of the three flights. I was exhausted like the others, found a tree, leaned against it, finished what was left of my water, and tried to stay upright. The meat wagon turned around, came back to me. Some of the boys were in the ambulance, encouraging me to climb in. I told them to go to hell—they could ride back, but I would finish by myself. The meat wagon took off to the base, dumped the load of men, came back, got behind me and followed me like a vulture the last five miles. When I finally got to the base, I went directly to the pub, backpack and all, gulped down two bottles of beer, and staggered to the barracks where I hit the bunk with all my equipment still on—the other men cat-calling and giving me the title of eager-beaver.

Me at age 19 in the U.S. Army Air Corps, 1938. Full dress (above), casual (next page).

Curtiss Hawk P6-E #39. Chanute Field, IL, 1938. The first P6-E I saw and fell in love with.

Douglas B-18. June, 1938.

Me standing in the bombardier's compartment getting ready to leave.

**Photos of the crash, the plane I was supposed to have been on
(this page and next).**

Air Corps Tech School of Photography, Denver, Colorado, 1938.

My photo class, 1938. I'm at the extreme left.

Me shooting Pictures from the rear cockpit of a Curtiss Falcon 01-A.

Me propping a P-26 (???)

Taking pictures in an airplane graveyard. I'm at the extreme right.

Me as a landlocked flying Cadet, U.S. Army Air Corps, 1944.

Wondering what to do, 1944.

The sea of Basic Trainer BT-13s I never got to fly, 1945.

CHAPTER FOUR

Sidetracked Again

From Amarillo, we expected to be shipped to pre-flight school. Instead, we were detoured to Gardner Field, California, where we learned that we were to be on a frozen status for an indefinite period of time. Apparently, this was because the war was beginning to turn in our favor, and the need for pilots had decreased dramatically. We, of course, were all very disappointed if not upset. In my case, I had made a very difficult decision in deciding to re-enlist with hopes of flying and seeing some action.

We were set up with our own squadron with five flights, appointed our own squadron commander and flight leaders, but under the supervision of a regular officer. We had no particular duties, just daily close order drill and constant inspection to keep us busy. We were allowed frequent passes, which many of the boys took advantage of. With nothing in particular to do, I checked to see if there were any paying jobs on the base. I hoped to find something to increase my income in addition to re-establishing my loan operation. We were being paid $50 a month as cadets, and this I sent home to my mother along with whatever I could from the loan operation. The only job I could get was working in the kitchen part time for $50 per month, so I took it.

After several months at Gardner, the boys were getting restless and complaining about not being allowed to start pre-flight. This built up to such a pitch, the Cadet squadron as a whole decided to mutiny and demanded a hearing with the base commander. We all were instructed to meet in the auditorium for a talk from him. He was not too pleased with our actions and told us in no uncertain terms to get back to our barracks, settle down, and behave ourselves. We were on a frozen status and would stay that way until the Air Corps decided otherwise.

After the meeting, I decided to go to the commander by myself and give him the message that all the men either wanted him to give us a definite answer when we would go into pre-flight, or transfer the entire squadron to the infantry. He asked me what my thoughts were since I was the old man of our squadron (at that time, 25 years old). I told him I felt the same way; I could not stand the inactivity. He was very sympathetic and understood our frustration. He informed me this last group had passed the highest standards and requirements of any previous Cadets and would remain on hold. Also, with the war turning in our favor, fewer pilots were being lost in aerial warfare than had been anticipated; however, we were being held in reserve in case of any reversals.

About mid-1944, we transferred to Douglas Air Base at Douglas, Arizona, right on the Mexican boarder. This was a basic training facility with BT-13s. We did eventually get to preflight the planes every day before flights, but that is as far as we got. This was an improvement over Gardner where all we did was march around all day.

In early 1945, I received a call from home that my mother was becoming ill. I got a 10 day pass and managed to get home partially by military planes on cross country flights and the rest of the way hitch-hiking. By the time I reached Omaha, my mother had been returned home from a short stay in the hospital. She had not been in very good health for some time, but seemed to be somewhat stabilized. I was not told of her true condition. The night before I left to return to Douglas, Arizona, I took her out to dinner. After dinner she remarked that I would probably not see her alive again. I attributed this remark to the typical Italian fatalistic way of thinking and lightly dismissed it. Had I known the truth, I would had stayed home and no doubt faced courtmartial for being AWOL, absent without leave.

In early August of 1945, I received another call from a cousin in Omaha who informed me that my mother had been taken to the hospital and had surgery, and I should get home as soon as possible. Also, the operation was not successful, and the doctor was going to perform another one. I objected, knowing that two major surgeries so close together can be fatal.

I immediately went to my squadron commander, an ex-insurance agent, and told him of my emergency. He was completely indifferent, said I could not have a pass. I was stunned. I told him to go to hell. At that particular time, I had sent all my funds home and had only 35 cents. I went to the Red Cross, asked for bus fare. They refused, giving no consideration to the emergency, my mother dying. With bus fare, I a least knew I would get home at a definite time. If I had to hitch-hike, it could take three to five days. Without an emergency pass, I could not get hops on military aircraft. I had only one means left, hitch-hike with 35 cent in my pocket.

Within an hour after the phone call, I left the base AWOL. Nobody tried to stop me. I got out on the highway and fortunately, during the war, people would pick you up if you were in uniform whereas before the war you would have had a problem getting rides. I was on the move constantly, every minute of the day and night. I got many more short lifts than long ones. It took me three and a half days to get home; I used 25 of my 35 cents for a couple of doughnuts and a cup of coffee. That was all I ate in that period.

I arrived in Omaha at 10:00 P.M. and went straight to the hospital. I found my mother in an oxygen tent, semi-conscious. I will never know if she recognized me. I stayed by her side in the hospital for three days and nights until she passed away within a few days of my birthday. Her prediction was almost true.

During the three days and nights I sat with my mother, the doctor who had performed the operations avoided me. I found out that he had left town the day I arrived. He knew that I knew he had performed two major surgeries in ten days—and without my legal consent. The human body cannot stand that kind of shock. I was infuriated. I found out he could have waited at least 30 days before the next operation.

After final arrangements had been completed and my mother laid to rest, I remained a few days before returning to Douglas Air Base. I was waiting for the doctor to return from out of town. I had found out why he'd performed two major surgeries in ten days: *He had to be at a golf tournament somewhere in the country.* So, without proper consent, he'd gone ahead anyway. I was enraged at what he had done. I went to his office and demanded to see him. The nurse refused to admit me. I pushed her aside, entered his office in a rage. He had heard me outside of the room, and when I went in he was sitting at his desk, his head bowed, his arms crossed. I shouted at him: "What was the cause of my Mother's death?" He did not respond. "Answer me!" I shouted. No answer. "She died of surgical shock, am I right?" He mumbled something, tears coming out of his eyes, and answered: "Yes." I cursed him. I wanted to grab him by the neck and strangle him. But I restrained myself, forced myself to leave.

A few days later I left to return to Douglas Air Base, this time on the bus. As I entered the Base and was walking along the path to the barracks, my commanding officer was approaching in a Jeep. He stopped to say something, but I continued to walk ahead. He called out, so I stopped. He did not threaten me, but remarked: "Is your mother all right? How is she?" I glared at him and answered: "She is dead, satisfied?" He said nothing, drove off, and never pressed charges. And I never saluted him thereafter.

August 11, 1945, my birthday, I was 26 years old. If I did not get into flight training 6 months before I became 27, I would automatically be transferred into pre-flight for the beginning of pilot training. Well, when the war was over in 1945, we were discharged 7 months before I was 27, one month too soon.

I returned home to Omaha and went back to the tool and die trade at the same factory where I had worked before. I was not satisfied with this, left and bought a partnership in a large gas station. I did this for a year, sold out, then had to decide what to do.

It was late 1946. I have thought about it many times and cannot figure out why I did not get back into aviation. I did start flying again, however. I had saved enough to purchase a 1947 Luscombe 8E, my first airplane, NC2464K. It was a sweet little airplane, I flew it a lot.

By early 1948—more specifically, April 1st, 1948, April Fools Day (an appropriate relationship)—I decided to start my own tool and die operation. I sold my car and used what savings I had, rented a small space large enough for a few machines, and started out by myself. Within a few months, I hired a helper; by the end of the first year I had three employees. With the business growing, I sold my little Luscombe to buy more machines—that hurt a lot. But I knew I would get another plane as soon as I could afford to.

We were cramped for space, so in mid-1949 I rented a 2,500 square foot building. The owner of the building was the largest manufacturer of hair accessories in the country. His plant is where I had learned the tool and die trade. He was angry because I had quit and would not return. He contacted my suppliers and told them not to give me credit. He called my machinery dealer and bank and tried to persuade them to shut me off. After all, he was the great white father (as he was called in Omaha), a county board member, and exercised much authority. My suppliers were upset at his actions, a multi-millionaire trying to prevent a young man from starting his own business. When he saw that I was beginning to do pretty well, he would not renew my lease—which expired in early 1951—and tried to force me to buy it at twice what it was worth. I had an appraisal and offered him 50% over the market value to avoid having to move. He would not accept my offer and forced me out.

I had already made plans to build my own 4,000 square foot building. In fact, it was under construction within a few days after he terminated my lease; I did have the 30 days he was required to give me. In that thirty days, with a large crew on the new building, I was able to move in time to beat his deadline.

At this point in the story, I feel I should inject a reminder of what this is all about. All of the events in the story are related and directly revolve around my obsession and ultimate goal in life—acquiring, somehow, a Curtiss Hawk P6-E, in my opinion the most beautiful airplane ever built. This all began in the mid-1930s when I built models of the plane. Through all the years, as I tried to accomplish that dream, there were frequent roadblocks and adversities beyond anyone's imagination.

Within two years after constructing the new building, I doubled its size. I now had 25 employees and was in metal stamping, contract manufacturing, and screw machine operation. Of the 25 employees, 16 were toolmakers. Then the first act of subterfuge occurred. I had employed two young boys directly out of high school as apprentices. I took them under my wing and gave them special instructions because they both had the ability to become excellent toolmakers. After several years, they became distant. At the same time I lost a few customers. While working for me the last two years of their employment, they had set up a shop, contacted my customers, and cut prices. One day they both walked into my office, informed me they were leaving, thanked me with an air of sarcasm for paying them well enough to start their own shop.

Omaha was not, and still is not, a heavy industrial manufacturing center. My shop was the first legitimate tool and die operation in the area; I was the only source for training toolmakers. Whenever a major company moved into Omaha, I would shudder. The first mass exodus happened when Western Electric built a huge plant. They contacted me with the pretense of surveying my facility and manpower to place orders. They visited my small plant, asked how many toolmakers I had, then assured me I would hear from them very soon. They obtained the names of 14 of my men, contacted them at home, offered them wages and benefits I could not afford in a small shop, and hired the entire group, leaving me with two men. I called the plant manager at Western Electric and expressed my thoughts about what they had done. He was sarcastic, asked if I had any men left so he could take them also—including me. I called the Omaha Chamber of Commerce to no avail. And this was not the end. Every few years, as I trained new men, the same act of deceit would be repeated throughout my entire business career. I will not go into detail on every case, but will mention a few of those I can remember and the number of men they took:

Control Data—12 men
EPE—14 men
American Meter—5 men
Snow Corp—4 men
Western Electric—l4 men
Continental Can—4 men

There were more than 50 such cases, many of which involved my men starting their own tool and die shops. There are about ten shops, all my ex-men. And so it went year after year. It takes 10 to 15 years to train a tool and die maker. I was the school.

By 1952, my heart was aching to have another airplane and to fly. The operator of North Omaha Airport, a small airport, had sold a Stinson Wagon to that party who had forced me out of my first building and took a Fairchild 24 with a 145 Warner engine in trade. Soon as I heard about it, I rushed out to the airport to try to buy it. It was a beautiful airplane. It had been custom built for Hoagy Charmical, the songwriter, who had named the ship "Stardust," after his hit song. It had a full-length engine cowling flush back to the windshield like a G Model Staggerwing. After much haggling, we agreed on a price that was too much, but he carried back a balance of the sale price, and I was not in a very good position to arbitrate any further.

What a beautiful little airplane. Flew like a dream. I worked day and night, but managed to fly it quite often. Then disaster struck. I always worked late by myself, would knock off around 10:30 P.M. to eat at an Italian restaurant owned by a good friend of mine (I was still single at that time). It was Saturday night. Two brothers were bartenders, and we became friends. At closing time, they asked if I would take them for an airplane ride the next day, Sunday. I told them I was pretty tired and had to work all day, but they insisted, so I agreed.

They showed up Sunday afternoon. I got the plane out, and they got in. I hadn't really noticed that they were both a little on the tipsy side, so I taxied out and took off. Within a few minutes we were over downtown Omaha. One brother, Don, was in the front with me, and the other, Bob, was in the back seat. Bob tapped me on the shoulder and informed me in no uncertain terms that he had to urinate. To lean forward to talk to me, he had taken his seat belt off. I told him we would be going back to the airport in a few minutes, but he wouldn't accept waiting and said that if I didn't go down immediately, he would pee all over the inside of the airplane.

At that moment I looked down and saw a grass strip, the South Omaha airport, just ahead. I was not familiar with the field, but told Bob to hold on; we would be on the ground in a few minutes. What a prediction! I was approaching from the north, and since the wind was out of the southeast, I planned a straight-in approach. There was a strong cross wind, and I had my left wing down to counteract drift. At the end of the strip there was a row of tall trees on the approach side of a road on the edge of the airport, so I had to come in pretty high to clear the trees, then I could side-slip to lose altitude. Just as we cleared the trees, Don in the front seat yelled out. At the same time I saw a power line. It was stretched across the end of the strip at telephone pole height and hadn't been visible before we'd cleared the trees. I hit full throttle and pulled up, but too late. With the left wing down and the long extended landing gear strut of a Fairchild, the left tire hit the wire, snapped it. The cable lashed upwards and out in front of the ship. I was moving ahead with enough speed to remain airborn, but the prop caught the power cable and wrapped it around the engine. When the airplane reached the end of the cable, it whiplashed us 180 degrees around. From fifty feet in the air, we crashed to the ground—ripping off both wings, the engine and mount all the way back to the firewall. The ship ended up on the firewall, tail straight up in the air, the cable around the engine throwing sparks, gas running out of the tanks onto ground.

When the airplane was snapped around 180 degrees to the right, the force jerked me to the left. My head struck the tubing over the left window, splitting my head open and knocking me unconscious for seven hours.

On the ground, the few people who witnessed the crash were, at first, unsure whether to try to get us out with the sparks flying around all that gas. They finally braved it. Since the plane was leaning somewhat to the pilot side, I was on the bottom of the heap. Don in front, on top of me, was only scratched; they got him out first. Bob in the back seat had not been knocked out, but he had not re-fastened his seat belt and had been thrown forward, hitting his face on the back of the front seat, and was covered with blood. They got him out, stood him on his feet, and proceeded to dig me out of the wreck. By now, the ambulance had arrived and hauled me to the hospital. When I finally awoke seven hours later, Don was sitting on a chair by my bedside and mumbled: "Thank God, I thought you were dead." I was able to ask how Bob was. Other than a smashed nose, he was OK. Later I found out that, after they'd dug him out of the wreck, he had disappeared. They'd found him standing behind a hangar, weaving back and forth, taking a pee . . .

One of the observers took us back to the North Omaha airport. I was pretty woosie. Don was OK. Bob had a big patch over his nose, the front of his shirt totally covered with blood. The operator of the airport, Angelo Bonacci, was in a panic—*not* because of the crash or our condition. He was hollering, as most Italians do, about who would pay the balance I owed on the Fairchild. In my daze, I couldn't believe this man. I tried to assure him that I would take care of it, but he wasn't satisfied. A friend of mine happened to be there, and Angelo had my friend sign a note as a witness to my statement that I would pay the balance owed to him.

And this was not the end; the power company sued me for the damage to their cable. Now the Italian in me came out. I went to the company headquarters. I happened to know one of the top officials; he flew and had a company airplane at the municipal airport. We had quite a heated discussion. I threatened to countersue them for having a hazardous installation at that airport. They backed off and canceled the lawsuit.

[*Footnote:* Two more planes hit the cable after it had been replaced two different times, killing two people. *Then* they buried the cable underground. I guess the man upstairs decided to keep me around so I could accomplish my dream of the Curtiss Hawk P6-E.]

Getting back to business, I was at the second shop location from 1951 to 1964, but could not expand further because I was surrounded by other buildings that restricted my growth. This present building was 8,000 square feet. I located a 22,000 square foot building in another part of town and moved once more. With this larger space, I built my tool and die operation to 20 men. From 12 metal stamping presses, I increased that department to 42 punch presses, got into plastics, set up four plastic injection molding machines. I was now up to 40 employees.

Once again, in 1954, I felt the strong urge to have another airplane and fly. I had to sell the pretty little Luscombe and had wrecked the beautiful Fairchild. I wanted something bigger and faster—a Spartan Executive. I found one, Serial #3. It was a great airplane, and I put about 250 hours on it. The previous owner had been a military pilot. He'd taken the wheel out and had put a stick in it. This was great, my kind of flying. But, alas, another problem . . .

In spite of that other Italian, Angelo, I returned to the North Omaha airport as my base for the Spartan. One day when taking off—after I'd previously put well over 200 hours on it—I heard a bang, almost like an explosion. Angelo, on the ground, called me on the radio and informed me that the right gear had partially retracted, then had fallen down. I'd already checked the light on the dash and could see that the gear was not up. I flew around for a while, shaking the airplane, stalling it, wiggling it, jerking it—anything to get the locking pin in. The gear was dangling and swaying. I made several slow passes across the field for verification that the gear appeared to be stationary. I finally gave up, made as slow as possible right wing down approach, touched down on the right wheel, cut power, and waited—holding my breath—as I held the left wing up and let it settle on the right wheel. As I rolled out, the gear stayed up. I remained on the runway, did not try to turn.

We inspected the gear-elevating mechanism. On the first three Spartans, bicycle chain and sprockets were used. The weight of the gear was too much for this flimsy arrangement. We repaired and replaced the chain with new ones on both sides. It lasted for a while, then happened again. We repaired it again. I had called Spartan Aircraft about converting the unit to the same arrangement they used on all the subsequent models, but I felt it too costly at the particular time.

Well, after what happened later, it would not have been. I was going into Meigs Field in downtown Chicago. As I lowered the gear, another bang; another chain broke. This time I was neither as lucky nor as skillful. On touch down the left gear collapsed. The ship spun around to the left, skidded off the runway, ended on the rim of the lake. I had cut the engine before touch down, and there were no sparks or fire. I climbed out madder than hell and stood by the ship. But once again the man upstairs had kept me in one piece again to get the Hawk project going.

Butler Aviation in Chicago repaired the airplane. I took it home, sure that everything being repaired with all new parts would solve the problem. Guess again! A few months later, it happened once more. I wired the gear down, took it to Spartan Aircraft, had them fix it, brought it home, and sold it. Many years later I saw it at Antique Airfield. John Turgen had acquired it.

All through the years up to 1960, the Hawk was becoming more of an obsession. With the business stabilized, I had time to start research. I began placing adds in *Trade-A-Plane* and many aviation magazines. I called every military air base in the country. I contacted every aviation historian I could track down, called every airplane junkyard I could locate. I contacted the Antique Airplane Association, Experimental Aircraft Association, War Birds, Smithsonian, and Air Force Museum. As a result of my advertising, I began to receive calls and letters from collectors and antiquers all over the country who shared the same dream: to acquire a Curtiss Hawk P6-E. Many had been researching for years, had no luck, and had come to the conclusion that there was not one to be found. One gentleman, Neil November of Richmond, Virginia, sent me a large package of correspondence covering a period from early l953 to mid 1967—fifteen years of trying to find or have a P6-E built. He contacted companies that had built vintage aircraft for movies. They informed him that it was difficult if not impossible to build a Hawk, and that the major problem was finding a Curtiss Conqueror V-1570 engine. He finally gave up and sent me all his information. Neil November's experience was typical of many collectors.

During the early years of research, I included in my advertising offers to purchase any original parts, pieces, engines, or anything that might have come off a P6-E. The most critical item was an original engine in case I found an airplane without its engine. By l964, I had managed to acquire parts of engines, partial engines, and hit the jackpot in finding one complete direct drive engine and all parts for another direct drive engine. I'd also found a complete geared engine and crank cases for three more. These came from all over the country—from Maine, Florida, Kansas, New Hampshire, and Michigan. The complete direct drive engine I found in Maine. It was in a speedboat, and I had to buy the boat to get the engine. Fortunately, all parts are interchangeable on both geared and direct drive engines.

In January of 1969, I acquired the second major item: an original lower left wing panel off P6-E #32-260. It still had the fabric on it with all the markings, lettering, and stars. It had been salvaged by a fellow named Ed Stringfellow, a World War II fighter pilot who was operating a lumber yard in Leeds, Alabama.

In a town not too distant from Leeds was a trade school that had the Hawk to instruct students in aircraft structure. Stringfellow knew of the aircraft and was keeping his eye on it with the intention of acquiring and restoring it. One day he got a frantic call that the school had decided to get rid of the plane. They'd taken it out of the school building, had thrown the wings in a pile with the fuselage, and were going to burn it. Stringfellow rushed to the site, but got there in time to save only the one lower left wing panel. Needless to say, he was outraged that the only Hawk known to be in existence at that time had been foolishly destroyed. He took the wing panel to his lumber yard and hung it from the ceiling where it remained for years until he saw my ads for Hawk parts. He too had the dream of owning one, but had given up. He wrote to me and offered to sell me the wing; the same day I got his letter I had a truck on the way to Leeds to pick it up. Many years later, aviation historian Bob Cavanaugh gave me a set of pictures of Curtiss Hawk P6-E Serial #32-260 when it had crashed. And that is another story.

Back in 1932, at Selfrige Field, where P6-Es of the 17th Pursuit Squadron were stationed, a reserve Major with 169 total hours had never flown one. He, in airplane #60, the last two digits of #32-260, and another officer in another P6-E went out to practice formation flying. Apparently the Major had not reviewed the operator's manual. They were at 3,000 feet when he decided to perform a roll. Part way through the roll, the ship fell off into an inverted flat spin. The Major bailed out, and the plane crashed upside down in a corn field. When he'd taken off, the belly tank had been full of gas. Had he read the manual, he would have known not to perform aerobatics in a P6-E with a full belly tank—the center of gravity becomes critical. The belly tank is only for cross country flights; no maneuvers permitted except when the tank is empty. This was confirmed recently by the engineering officer at Selfrige at that time, 89-year-old Colonel Paul Jacobs whom I met with in December of 1992. His P6-E was #32-256 or #56.

For several years, I had kept the wing in a secured room where no one was allowed without my permission. When I was out of town on business, an antique airplane buff visited Omaha. He had heard of the wing and wanted to see it. The office girl told him that only I could show it to him. He convinced her that he was a friend and knew I would not object. She let him into the storage room. He then did an unforgivable act: he cut half the fabric off the wing, I suppose for a souvenir. I never found out who he was.

Although the Hawk was my main obsession, I'd always had strong interest in another plane—a Gullwing Stinson SR-9—and hoped to have one someday. I had looked at several over the years and finally found an exceptional one, owned by an automobile dealer, in Williamsport, Pennsylvania. I had contacted him to try to buy the ship, but it was not for sale. I called him every six months or so to find out if he had changed his mind. Then one day two years later he called me and said he would sell me the Stinson, provided I would keep it permanently and not sell it to anyone. Should I decide to sell it, I was to give him first opportunity to re-purchase it. I agreed to his terms. I closed the deal in early 1964, brought it home, and still have it. I have been bombarded with calls year after year from people wanting to purchase it, but I will not sell it at any price, not in my lifetime. It is a beautiful, majestic aircraft, a Cadillac of the air. It is identified with me and part of me. And I have a room full of trophies N17179 carried home.

After giving up the Spartan Executive, I always wanted another 200-mile-an-hour airplane. The opportunity arose in October of 1965. My old friend at the North Omaha airport called me in a panic one Friday morning to inform me that Piper Aircraft was closing out their final inventory of five 400 Commanches—just what I wanted. I called the sales manager at Piper. He told me they were all gone; however, he had not received a deposit on the last one, N8500P. I asked him how much the deposit must be, told him I would wire it immediately if there was a chance of getting that airplane. He agreed to hold it till 3:00 P.M. the next day. If the other deposit was not received by that time, the airplane was mine. And that is how I acquired N8500P. To relive the old days, I wanted an open cockpit biplane. During the summer of 1965 I located a 300HP Lycoming Stearman owned by Fred Schaffer of Indianapolis, Indiana. It had traveled with Bill Adams, the stunt pilot who had died in a crash when the prop on his 450 Stearman twisted off. Like the Stinson, it took a while to obtain the plane, but finally Fred called me, and the airplane was available. Ray Goss from West Bend, Wisconsin, picked up the Stearman, flew it to Cliff Ducharme's shop, and completely refurbished the airplane as it is today. And it, too, has carried home a room full of trophies.

Continuing my search for the Curtiss Hawk into 1969, almost ten years, I was becoming totally frustrated and impatient. I had traveled and chased down rumors all over the country with no results. I had received virtually hundreds of phone calls and letters from people everywhere who wanted to help and were excited at the possibility of a real, flying P6-E. I had been to the Air Force Museum at Dayton, Ohio, gathering information, photographs, and all historical information they had available—which wasn't a great deal. They did have two rolls of microfilm which I borrowed and made a duplicate set. This provided only a small amount of information and some drawings, which were not near enough to build the real airplane. The Smithsonian provided nothing.

Then an unbelievable stroke of luck. On August 28, 1969, I received a phone call from Hank Leslie of Fort Worth, Texas. He had seen my many ads for P6-E information in *Trade-A-Plane* and asked if I was serious about building the Hawk if I could not find one. I assured him that I was. Then he informed me that he had a complete set of one-quarter scale factory blueprints, would send them to me, but I must provide him with progress pictures and information. I agreed.

I was getting to the end of the line. There was only one piece of information I decided to check into. I questioned the credibility of this remote possibility. At this stage of my endeavor, I could not stop, but I also could not go on forever. Many others had tried for years and had failed, and I was on the brink of failure, too. But failure was not acceptable. I would check out this questionable rumor, and if it seemed realistic enough, I would pursue it. If the rumor proved to be false, I must then decide to try to build a Hawk now that I had drawings. I would not settle for a replica; it would have to be a real, factory built airplane.

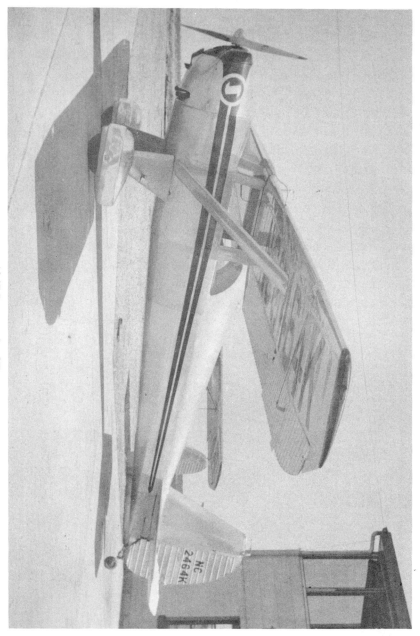

1947 Luscombe 8E

Fairchild 24 "Stardust"

1937 Stinson SR-9 "Gullwing"

1965 400 Comanche

1941 Stearman PT-17

1975 Cessna 310R

Curtiss Hawk P6-E #60, which crashed on August 25, 1932—168 hours (next three pages). I have the left lower wing panel.

CHAPTER FIVE

The Rumor

During the Thirties, The United States was supposed to have given the Commanding General of the Bolivian Air Force a Curtiss Hawk P6-E. Some years later he was killed in a coup while flying in a helicopter that was blown up in the air. The General's wife left Bolivia, came to the United States, re-married, and was living in Washington, D.C.

After extensive searching, I located her and managed to get her phone number. I contacted her and told her my reason for calling. She confirmed that indeed the United States had given her husband, the General, an airplane. She did not know what kind it was, but thought it might still be in Bolivia.

She and her husband had lived on a ranch some distance from Santa Cruz. I drew a map as she described how to get there. The airplane was supposed to be crated in a barn located a short distance from the house they had lived in. The ranch was several hours drive from Santa Cruz, but would not be too hard to find because it had an air strip. Farmers in the area would know about it and could direct me to the location.

Another rumor had a Hawk, the model unknown, sunken in the ocean along the coast of Columbia, South America. Still another had one buried in a river outlet to the sea at the southern end of Guatemala. There might be a Hawk in Lima, Peru, one somewhere in Paraguay, Honduras, Timbucktu, wherever. All through the years, I kept a log of hundreds of phone calls all over the United States, Canada, Mexico, Central and South America. I talked to people in all walks of life, hoping for any bit of information helpful in my quest.

The time had come to make the decision to end this madness or make one final effort to investigate all these questionable rumors, as remote as they might be. Ten years had gone by, but I could not and would not bring myself to give up. The challenge, the obsession, had grown out of control, and it angered me that 45 P6-E Hawks had been destroyed. The remaining one at the Air Force Museum in Dayton was such an outrageous restoration, way below my standards. Much of it was fiberglass held together with wood screws, inaccurate fairings, the engine inoperable, and the airplane not flyable. A sole example of such a historical aircraft should have been meticulously restored.

In late 1969, I began to plan the excursion into the unknown, to venture forth wherever the rumors took me, to go where no one had been, and either realize my dream or terminate it. Um . . . sounds like *Star Trek*—and I might add, some of my experiences were just as bizarre.

By January of 1970, I had my routing and schedule complete. My search would begin in Mexico. The first stop would be at Torenna, on to Guadalauara, San Luis Potosi, and finally Mexico City. From there, take an airliner to Guatemala, Central America, continue on to Lima, Peru, La Paz, Bolivia, Concepción, Paraguay, and finally Bogota and Cali, Columbia. The countries in South America had the strongest possibilities, so I decided to by-pass the places in Mexico and search them on returning.

My airlines and flights had been arranged in Omaha by a travel agency, and I assumed they would be on major airlines that serviced Central and South American countries.

The first leg of my journey from Omaha to Mexico City was booked on Braniff Airlines. That was quite a ride. I sat in the first row behind the pilot's cabin. Before the flight departed, the Captain came out of the cockpit, walked down the aisle greeting everyone, very friendly guy. When he came back, he stopped and welcomed me aboard, wanted to know my destination. I told him Central and South America. He asked the purpose of my trip—business or otherwise. I told him, jokingly, I was on a Hawk Safari, was searching the world for a Curtiss Hawk P6-E. He excitedly invited me into the cabin, and I sat in the jump seat. The airliner was a Boeing 707.

He had given me his business card; I can't find it so do not remember his name. He sat in the Captain's seat, but turned around facing me, told the copilot to take over. We taxied out to the runway. The Captain took over for a moment, punched some buttons. The plane took off, and the Captain told the copilot to take over, once again, turned around to me and we talked airplanes and antiques all the way to Mexico City.

I had a few hours layover in Mexico City. The next leg of my trip was to Guatemala City. I took my time locating the departure gate. The waiting area was crowded, and I assumed the airliner—a shiny new DC-9 jet—was my flight (since its destination was Guatemala City) and would be filled. When the flight was called and passengars began boarding, I didn't check my ticket for the flight number, just got in line. When I got to the agent, he started to remove the ticket, but stopped abruptly. "*Señor,* this is not your flight. This is Aero Mexico. Your airline is Aero Guatemala, that airplane over there."

While waiting for the flight to board, I had stood gazing out the window. Next to that beautiful DC-9 was parked its predecessor, a dilapidate old four-engine propeller-driven DC-4, vintage early 1940s. There is nothing wrong with an old airplane that has been well maintained and kept in presentable appearance, especially as an airliner. Earlier, as I stared at the DC-4, I thought, God, I sure as hell wouldn't want to ride in that thing. The airplane looked as if it had been through a massive hailstorm or some overly angry mechanic had worked the ship over with a ball peen hammer. There was as much dented surface as smooth, and the entire plane was dirty. The engines were leaking oil—large puddles on the ramp, engine cowlings and belly covered with dripping oil.

My flight's scheduled departure time had passed. That new shiny DC-9 had been gone an hour. My flight was supposed to have left at the same time. The airline agent informed me that there was a slight mechanical problem but: "Do not worry, *Señor,* the plane will be ready very soon." Another classic statement to record for posterity . . .

Mechanics were scurrying all around the ship, talking back and forth excitedly, giving instructions, whatever. The pilot had been trying to start the engines for over an hour. Mechanics would open and close the engine cowlings repeatedly and motion for the pilot to try again. The agent kept me well informed too frequently: "Very soon *Señor.*"

I suddenly realized the waiting area was empty. I was alone except for a Catholic priest sitting in a chair nearby. He stood up and went over to the window. I guessed that he might be the only other passenger on my flight. I thought: "Well, the good Lord is still with me—at least I have a priest to administer the last rites, provided he survives." If only I survived. And since I, too, was Catholic, I would do my best to put him at rest.

I introduced myself to the priest since he and I were to be the only passengers on the flight. He was a missionary and had been in the Guatemala City area hills for a number of years teaching the natives farming, gardening, and religion. He was a very friendly and personable fellow.

I continued to watch out the waiting area window, hoping for some positive progress on the DC-4. After about two and a half hours, three of the engines were finally running and the fourth one belched a cloud of smoke and oil, fighting desperately to prove that it could run. The priest was very quiet, also gazing out the window, so I assumed he was praying. His prayers were answered. The fourth engine coughed and sputtered into life, the mechanics excitedly waving a victory sign to the pilot. The agent informed us that the flight was ready to leave, gave us special attention, and led us all the way out to the airliner. We entered, and being the only two on board, had a good selection of seats.

I always felt the safest place on an airliner is at the rear, near the tail, so I headed for that area. My new friend, the Priest, wanted to sit behind the pilot's cabin in the first row. We compromised and settled for over the wing, the most comfortable place in case of rough air. Also, I could keep my eyes on the engines much better from this location.

I glumly settled into my seat and began to mentally review my future conversation with the travel agency back home. My Priest friend had gone up to the cockpit for a few minutes to talk to the crew, whom he knew from many previous trips, probably to take their confessions. He came back, sat down, and informed me that we were ready to go. I tightened my seat belt. Now it was my turn to pray.

I told the Priest about my disappointment of not being on the *jet* plane that left three hours earlier with a flight time of one and one half hours to Guatemala City. Our schedule was four hours. He joyfully remarked: "This is great fun. I like roughing it in this old plane. It's a longer ride, and you get to see more." I now knew he had been in the hills too long. I did not respond, but was soon to know what he meant when he said we would see more.

We taxied out to the runway and took off in a cloud of smoke and streaming oil. I had tightened my seatbelt earlier, but now I wondered if I should leave it loose for a fast exit. We climbed out of the airport and leveled off at a fairly low altitude. I had worn a suit because I was not concerned about the heat; I had taken for granted that I would be in a modern air-conditioned airliner. Once again, the travel agency came to mind. The Priest had removed his coat and reaffirmed his love for this roughing it. I mumbled something and began to disrobe to keep cool.

We were airborne for about half an hour and still at a very low altitude. I wondered about this and mentioned it to the Priest. He remarked that they always flew this low. My guess was the engines did not have enough power to go higher. It was beginning to get rough. We bounced, creaked, and groaned through the air, it seemed forever. The engines had been throttled back, possibly to make the ride more comfortable, but I really think to keep the pieces together. The Priest's earlier remark that we would see more was true. We were bouncing over the tops of hills and mountains I felt I could reach out and touch. Scenic, but too close for comfort.

Dusk was settling in. The flight was approximately four hours late. My companion was carrying on a one-sided conversation when he interrupted himself and informed me that we had arrived at our destination. Somehow, we landed without incident, taxied to the terminal, and deplaned—me with a great feeling of relief. We walked toward the terminal building; a short distance away was parked that beautiful slick Jet airliner. Once again my thoughts turned to the travel agency in Omaha.

My Priest friend had someone waiting to pick him up. We said our farewells and wished each other good luck in our individual ventures. It was late in the evening, getting dark. I was anxious to get to a hotel and turn in so I could get an early start next morning. After a lengthy wait, I got a cab, drove into Guatemala City, and checked into the *Hotel El Camino Real*.

CHAPTER SIX

Guatemala and the Captain

The next morning, I arose early, had a quick breakfast, returned to my room, and planned my schedule for the day. My first step was to contact the U.S. Air Attaché. I explained my purpose for being in Guatemala and asked if he knew of any old aircraft anywhere in the country. I also told him of a P-26 fuselage that was supposed to be at the extreme southern end of the country near an airstrip cut through the jungle not too far from the ocean and the possibility of a Curtiss Hawk P-1 in the bay area. I had pictures and a map of the location of the P-26 fuselage.

He was not aware of any of what I was looking for and suggested we meet with members of the Guatemala Air Force. This included officers and mechanics who traveled the country and might know of any old aircraft.

We went to the air base headquarters and met with the commanding General of the Air Force. After introductions, I explained my mission. He had heard rumors of old aircraft in Guatemala, but knew of nothing specific. He suggested I talk to other personnel. He was very gracious, spoke good English, and we had a rather lengthy conversation. We left the office, the Commandant with us, strolled outside to view his Air Force. There were a few C-47 transports, a number of T-6s and P-51 Mustangs. They had no jet fighters. By now we had imposed on the Commandant for several hours. I thanked him for his patience and consideration and excused myself so he could attend to his own activities. He was a tall, handsome gentleman and had a humorous side in all our conversation. As we parted, he smiled and remarked: "*Señor*, since you are looking for old and antique aircraft, why don't you purchase the entire Guatemala Air Force"; practically every ship on the field was pre-World War II vintage.

After parting with the Commandant, I spent the rest of the day on the air base talking to officers and enlisted personnel, hoping for some concrete information on the two aircraft for which I was searching. One officer had a Waco biplane stored in the back of a locked hangar. I did not get to see it; no one knew the model, but it was not for sale.

A problem I had not anticipated was communication. I could speak

Italian and assumed I would have no problem understanding Spanish. I could speak some Spanish, but their manner of speaking is rapid and staccato, and I had trouble understanding. I found out very soon that Italian and Spanish might seem much the same, but to carry on a comprehensible conversation is difficult if not impossible. When available, U.S. military personnel translated for me, or if I was alone, I did the best I could with a combination of what Spanish I knew, sign language, and drawings.

The first day of my "safari" passed into evening. I returned to my hotel after dinner and, before retiring, outlined my activity for the next day.

Morning came quickly. The previous day, I'd been told of two Americans operating flying services at the Guatemala City airport. One of them, Tom Keane, had been on the field many years, and I hoped he might know as much about old aircraft in Guatemala as anyone.

The airport was well secured by fences and armed guards. I had rented a car, and as I approached a gate leading into the field, an armed soldier stopped me and would not allow me to pass. I tried to explain, with mixed Italian and Spanish, that I wanted to go to the opposite side of the airport where the private flying services were. He couldn't understand me and angrily kept waving me away. I would not leave. I made a drawing showing him where I wanted to go and mentioned Tom Keane's name. He broke into a big grin and said "*Si, Si, Señor*, you go." He then opened the gate and allowed me to enter, pointing excitedly in some direction or other which I determined to be right across the middle of the field—nice short cut; planes were taking off and landing. I decided to do otherwise and drove around the perimeter of the field to the opposite side where the flight services operated.

After more inquiries, I located Tom Keane and was relieved to find that he was someone I could communicate with. Surprisingly, he had an aunt in Omaha, my home town, and that established a friendlier atmosphere. He had been in Guatemala many years and liked being there very much. Life was a lot simpler and the cost of living less expensive. He operated a crop-dusting and charter flying service and was very familiar with the country. After casual conversation, I told him the purpose of my trip to Central and South America.

Tom recounted what information he knew. Back in the 1930s or 1940s, the United States had provided the Guatemala Air Force with a squadron of Boeing P-26 "Peashooter" pursuit planes. The Guatemalan pilots, although trained in the United States, could not seem to master this tricky little fighter. Tom told of the many P-26s that were crashed either on take-off or landing. He jokingly described how the pilots would either pull up too soon on take-off, stall, and crash or—when approaching to land—would aim at the field, dive at it, sometimes not level off soon enough, and crash into the ground. Others were lost in cross country flights.

As a result, even at this late date, he suggested there might be parts and possibly a complete airplane that had crashed in the jungles. He had known of one that went down in the hills near the city, but thought it had been found and taken to the United States a few years before my visit. Other than that, he knew of nothing in the immediate area. I had no special interest in a P-26 because I knew a few existed; however, part of the reason for my trip to Guatemala was to find one for another antique collector, Dick McWhorter of Prosser, Washington. He had told me of the P-26 fuselage near the jungle strip at the south end of the country and actually had a picture of himself standing beside it. As long as I was going to be in Guatemala, he asked if I would see if it were still there. This friendly gesture on my part turned into a life-threatening experience.

It was approaching mid-morning, and not wanting to loose any more time, I asked Tom if he had a rental plane and pilot available. I wanted to check out the rumor of the Curtiss Hawk P-1 and find out if the P-26 fuselage was still where Dick McWhorter had seen it. Both were supposed to be in the same area.

Tom did not have a plane or pilot available; however, he contacted a young Guatemalan pilot who agreed to take me. After considerable customary negotiating, we agreed on a cost and prepared to leave.

The terrain was mountainous, and my pilot was not too excited about the course we were to fly. The plane was a Cessna 180. He was worried about getting high enough to clear the mountains. Tom assured him that it would not be a problem. We got in the airplane and took off. It was now close to noon. I don't recall the pilot's name. For the sake of identifying him, we will call him José. The flight was not very long. José could not speak one word of English. He was in his thirties, very congenial, and talked non-stop all during the flight. I couldn't respond, just ignored him while checking our flight course.

It was a long slow climb out of the airport to reach 10,000 feet to clear the mountains. We passed over the last range and began to descend to the lowlands that led to the Pacific ocean. At the base of the mountains, the terrain changed into jungle in every direction. José was uncomfortable flying over the jungle, more so than over the jagged mountains.

Halfway between the base of the mountains and the ocean, a distance of approximately 20 miles, I began to look for the air strip. José had held a good direct course, and I quickly saw a narrow runway buried in the jungle. We made a straight-in approach and landed—then all hell broke loose.

We had barely touched down and were rolling down the runway. Looking out the right window, I saw what looked like the Charge of the Light Brigade rushing at us out of the jungle. A group of guerrillas. Terrorists? I did not know what. We had barely stopped, and they immediately surrounded the airplane with machine guns and rifles. We could not taxi off, so José shut down the engine.

One who seemed to be in charge, rushed to the plane, jerked the cabin door open on my side, grabbed me by the arm, shouting for me to get out. As I deplaned, he pressed a pistol to my back, screaming all the while in Spanish. I think he was angry about something. He virtually dragged me out in front of the airplane, had me surrounded by six men dressed in battle gear and armed to the teeth with machine guns, ammunition belts, and hand grenades. These little fellows stood just far enough away from me so that the machine guns were about six inches from my chest. They glared at me in kind of an unfriendly way, to put it mildly, their fingers on the triggers. I heard one of them call the head man "Captain" and determined that these were Guatemalan soldiers fighting Rebels in the jungle.

After disposing of me, the head man went back to the airplane, shouting at José to get out, José shouting just as loudly at him. They stood on the runway arguing excitedly, José trying, I guessed, to explain why we were there. And now I began to wonder why I was there. It was not to seek out a P6-E Hawk; the rumor was for a P-1 Hawk, which was worth researching, but its existence was extremely doubtful. The main purpose was to find out for Dick McWhorter if the P-26 fuselage was still there.

The Captain and José entered a small shack a short distance away. They were gone for over an hour. By now I had been standing in the blazing hot sun for over two hours, not moving and hardly breathing lest my captors mistake any movement for an act of hostility and get trigger happy.

The Captain and José came out of the shack, still arguing steadily, neither letting the other complete his side of the conversation. The shack had a porch on the front of it supported by two posts, one at each end. Attached to one of the posts was a telephone. The Captain picked up the phone and was trying to get a call through, I found out later, to the Minister of Security in Guatemala City. He did not seem to have much luck; the phone system was not too efficient from this remote area. He eventually made contact, but had to wait for a return call from the Security department of the government.

While waiting for the call, he came over to me. He could speak understandable English and informed me that I had entered a war zone. They were fighting the Rebels in the adjacent jungle, and I was under arrest for penetrating a restricted area and the possibility that I was a spy for the Rebels.

José had informed him of my purpose for being there, to find an old airplane. The Captain was angry if not furious and was adamant in his stand not to allow me to go into the jungle where the P-26 fuselage was supposed to be. He was waiting to hear from the Minister Of Security to get clearance to release me. I then told him that I knew the Commanding General of the Guatemala Air Force, and he could contact him to confirm my innocence.

The afternoon had passed. I was still under guard, the Captain impatient and angry over my presence. I was to find out why a few days later. I had been standing in the hot sun almost six hours, still encircled by the soldiers. They did not seem bothered by the heat. It was late and would be getting dark soon, and José was getting nervous. He approached the Captain and heatedly told him we had to leave before it got too late since we had to fly over the mountains. He finally convinced the Captain to let us go. We were escorted back to the plane. As I climbed in, the Captain was expounding off to José, looked at me and angrily spoke in English: "*Señor*, stay away from here. Do not come back." I was to hear the same phrase in every country I visited in Central and South America.

We took off, returned to Guatemala City airport, arriving right at dark. All during the flight back, José was talking excitedly in Spanish, I guess to try to make me understand why we were unable to complete our mission. After we landed, we went directly to Tom Keane's office to tell him what had happened. José explained in Spanish, and Tom translated for me. The area we landed in was a highly-secured military zone and not accessible to anyone under any circumstances. José had argued that what I wanted to do was not military activity and would inconvenience no one.

The end result of the discussion between the two was that the Captain would, against his will, allow me to search the jungle area if I had a release from the Department of Security or War Department of Guatemala, headquartered in Guatemala City. This had to be in the form of a signed document by the Minister of Security. The Captain, however, demanded we not return even with the security release.

I thanked Tom for explaining the situation. He suggested I not pursue returning to the jungle strip any further, but research other parts of the country. I was puzzled. I felt I was not being told the whole story since his suggestion seemed more of a warning than advice.

I negotiated a settlement with José and asked if he would fly me back to the search area in the next day or so after I got the necessary permits and releases. He excitedly answered, in no way would he return. I would have to find someone else. Once again I was puzzled. His attitude also seemed to convey a warning. Ignorance *is* sometimes bliss.

I was determined to return. Early the next morning, I would go to the Federal Building in Guatemala City to meet with the Minister of Security, Minister of Defense, President, Dictator, or whoever it took to get clearance. I came all this distance and could not stop now. I had no difficulty in locating the government offices. The building was very imposing, typical of architecture of federal buildings in Central and South America. Along the front of the block-long building were stationed at least a dozen soldiers. I wondered if I was going to have a problem getting past them. As I climbed the many steps leading up to the entrance, two of the guards moved towards me and surveyed me. I greeted them in my best Spanish. They smiled, acknowledged my greeting, and allowed me to pass. I entered the building and looked for someone to direct me to the Department of Security. The huge lobby was deserted, no one in sight. Finally an enlisted man, a Sergeant, came out of one of the many offices surrounding the lobby. I stopped him, and after a few minutes of speaking Spanish as best I could, he understood what I wanted.

It turned out that he worked in the Ministry of Security. He led me up a long staircase to a second story balcony, motioned for me to have a seat and wait while he arranged a meeting with the proper official. He could speak a few words of English. "Five minutes, *Señor*, five minutes." Before I left the hotel that morning, I had called the American Air

Attaché, told him of my problem. He offered to call the Ministry of Security, whom he knew, and set up an appointment. I assumed he had done this, so I took for granted there would be no delay.

Five minutes went by. Out of the office came the Sergeant. "Five minutes, *Señor*, five minutes." I had gotten there at 9:00 A.M. hoping to get this matter taken care of as soon as possible so I could go back to the airport, find a plane and pilot, and have time to return to the jungle strip. The second five minutes passed. Once again here came the Sergeant: "Five minutes, *Señor*, five minutes." This fellow was very punctual. I began to wonder if he meant that he would return every five minutes or if the appointment was in five minutes.

The hours dragged by. I sat and walked and sat and walked. The faithful Sergeant, a short, robust, congenial, little fellow, reported to me every five minutes. It would soon be noon. My Sergeant then reported that the Minister had gone to lunch and when he returned, we would meet. I remembered that in Mexico and South America, lunch is a 2 P.M. to 4 P.M. siesta. I decided not to leave; I did not want to take the chance of missing him when he returned. The Sergeant had also left, but did return after two hours and continued his reporting schedule. I knew he meant well, but his perpetual "Five minutes, *Señor*, five minutes" was starting to wear on my patience. I tried to make him understand that he did not have to report to me every five minutes and keep running back and forth. "No, no, *Señor*, I must let you know when the Minister will be back."

The day was passing slowly and rapidly. It was 4:00 P.M.. There was no chance of seeing the Minister that day. I made the Sergeant understand that I could wait no longer and left. I immediately went to the U.S. Air Mission and told one of the officers of my problem. He suggested I contact the Commandant of the Air Force, who I had a good rapport with. He should have enough influence to expedite obtaining the permit and security clearance.

It was very late in the afternoon, but I decided to take a chance on finding the Commandant at the air base. Fortunately, he was still in his office. I explained my problem. Although I had waited most of the day to meet with the Minister of Security, he was unavailable. The Commandant deliberated for a short time. Since he was one of the highest ranking officials in the country, he had the authority to provide me with the clearance I needed. He prepared a note, affixed his signature, and assumed full responsibility for the contents. He also would inform the

Minister of Security the next day, so I could proceed with my plans and not loose another day.

The next morning I faced another problem: I had to find a pilot and plane to return to the jungle strip. I remembered someone had mentioned there was another American who bought and sold airplanes and operated a charter service and was based at the Guatemala City airport. I drove to the civilian side of the airport by way of the perimeter road and inquired of his whereabouts. Communicating with the Guatemalans was becoming tortuously exasperating, not withstanding the repeated loss of time whenever I tried to carry on a conversation.

I finally found my man. Between an office building and a tree was strung a fish net hammock. Laying luxuriously in it was a mass of a man. He appeared more like a whale that had been beached and deposited into the net. I wondered how he got into it and guessed that he had to roll over and fall to the ground to get out. I could understand him buying and selling airplanes, but wondered how he could get into one. It would have to be a good sized plane if he and I were to be in it together.

As I approached, I was greeted with a friendly welcome. The gentleman spoke with a heavy southern drawl and was obviously from the Southern states of the U.S.A. I introduced myself. He responded, informing me that his name was George Adler. He operated an air-taxi service, crop dusting, gave flight instruction, performed aerial photography, and Propaganda Commercial, whatever that was. He had been in Guatemala many years, and like Tom Keane, enjoyed living there.

There were very few Americans in this country, so George was curious about my presence. I explained why I was there, but did not bother to tell him what had happened the first few days. Just that I needed a plane and pilot to fly me to the southern coast. The only plane George had available was a twin Beech. To fly over the mountains, he would use only that airplane.

George had been in Central America long enough to have acquired some of the natives' habits, namely bartering. The flight was about an hour each way. He started out at $500, or $250 one way. I wondered about the one way figure. Italians are pretty good at bartering too— so, after lengthy good natured bargaining, we agreed to $225 for the round trip.

I was anxious to get going as quickly as possible. We had most of the day ahead of us and had sufficient time to fly to the coastal area and return before dark. I now told George of our destination. He was well acquainted with the area and air strip. He suggested it was not a very good idea to make this trip. After some, if not a lot, of prodding he reluctantly agreed to go. Again, from yet another person, a tone of apprehension and hint of warning.

We were soon airborne, climbing to the altitude necessary to clear the mountains. The flight over them was much more comfortable in the heavier twin than had been in the little Cessna. All the while, George told me of his life in this Central American country, a relaxed existence without the pressures of living in the U.S.A.

As we cleared the mountains I could see the runway ahead. Geroge descended, made a low pass over the field, circled, and began final approach to land. As we neared the end of the runway just before touch-down, I exclaimed: "Oh no, not again." Out of the jungle, here they came, the Charge Of The Light Brigade, that small army rushing at us. We rolled to a stop, but again were not allowed to turn off the runway. The soldiers encircled the airplane as before. I guessed they thought another stranger was in their midst, not knowing it could be me again. Oh Boy—

My friend, the same Captain, appeared in front of the plane and angrily motioned George to cut the engines, after which he shouted for us to deplane. I was first out, and as I opened the cabin door, I shrunk in size. The Captain recognized me, assumed the stance of a fighting cock, his hands on his hips, his body arched forward, his head protruding ahead of his body, then roared what I am surewere some choice expletives in Spanish. He was enraged and kept up a steady stream of vocabulary at me.

As George was exiting the plane, he stopped, wondering what the Hell was going on. Take two: the Captain grabbed me by the arm—this time he was nicer, did not have his pistol in my back—led me a short distance from the plane, shouted to his squad. Again they surrounded me with those ugly machine guns, the little fellows looking just as mean as before.

George finished his descent from the airplane, approached the Captain, and in Spanish asked what the problem was. I guessed the Captain was explaining my previous visit. George looked at me, perturbed, and remarked: "You didn't tell me you were here before." I shrugged my shoulders, said nothing. (No wonder my first flight instructor, Wolf Powell, called me Hardnose—I call it determination.)

George finally got the Captain calmed down enough to let him know

I had the necessary permits and clearance to go into the jungle. That in no way satisfied him. He came over to me, his face in mine, and in no uncertain terms stated: "*Señor*—You cannot go into thee jungle." I reminded him that I had clearance from the proper authorities. He screamed: "No, you cannot go." I questioned him: "Why not?" (Hard-nose again.) "Because I say you cannot go." He turned away, stomped around in a circle a few times, mumbling all the while. George stood nearby shaking his head.

My Captain friend came back to me, hands on his hips, and roared out: "*Señor*, you want to go to thee jungle, you want to go to thee jungle?" I answered: "Yes." He grumbled: "You want to go to thee jungle, you cannot go to thee jungle. I will take you to thee jungle. You want to go over there?—OK, we will go." All this while, we had not been given an explanation of his objections. We were to soon know—the hard way.

The squad disbanded. The Captain escorted George and me to the shack for a consultation. He wanted to know the precise location of the airplane fuselage. The original information and picture I had showed it near the military installation. It was not in that area, so I thought it might have been moved and disposed of in the jungle. The Captain, angry and impatient, led us to a narrow path leading into the wilderness. He was in front, I behind him, and big George following me. I told George he did not have to go along, but his curiosity had gotten the best of him. The path was barely wide enough for me to pass through. The Captain, much smaller, had no problem. However, George, as huge as he was, would have to fight his way through the brush and foliage bordering the path, but he insisted on going.

Just before we were to enter the passage, the Captain angrily instructed us in the procedure for following him. "*Señors*, you must walk very slow and put your feet exactly where I put my feet, but do not be too close behind me. Stop when I stop."

The Captain proceeded ahead very slowly. I waited to allow time for a separation of approximately fifteen feet, George repeating the distance between him and me, mumbling something or other. He was having a problem getting through. We could hear gunfire in the distance ahead, but kept going. The path twisted and turned; the Captain would stop and wait for me to come in sight behind him, I doing the same for George. We were about 300 yards into the jungle, moving very slowly, I watching where our leader was placing his feet and waiting for George to mate with my imprints. All the while the Captain was talking to himself in an abbreviated tone.

This playing tipy-toes was getting wearing, particularly on George. He stopped short and bellowed so the Captain ahead could hear: "Why the hell are we walking like this!" Our benefactor stopped in his tracks, turned his head towards us, and performed a pirouette that would make the world's greatest ballerina envious and retire in a state of awe. "*Señor*, you want to come in thee jungle, I try to tell you we cannot come here, but you want to come, so we come. Thees is a war zone, and we are fighting the Rebels in the jungle, and thees is a mine field—we can all be keeled."

George froze in his tracks—needless to say, so did I. I shouted to the Captain: "Why didn't you tell us before?" "*Señor*, you did not ask me eef thees was a mine field." I had already determined in previous conversations with Latins that they will only tell you what you specifically ask, but volunteer no more. Several times when I had asked why we could not enter the jungle, I should have asked if there were mine fields.

George let out a scream: "What the Hell are we doing here? I am getting out of here. No damn airplane is worth this." I shouted to the Captain to stop, we were going back. I, too, agreed that my life was worth more than an airplane, particularly one I was not interested in, just doing someone a favor. I wonder what I would have done if it had been a Curtiss Hawk P6-E. Now the Captain was furious. I had forced him into this search against his will. He had endangered his life, but I am sure ours weren't that important to him.

Now came a delicate maneuver. To return, we had to retrace our steps to avoid the mines. This meant that the Captain had to lead us out. To do this he had to get past both of us. He approached me, and clinging to my shoulders, lifted himself, swung around in back of me and lowered to the ground. Now he had to get past George. The Captain carefully tread his way to him fifteen feet away and stopped short. To get past this mountain of a man was going to be an operation in itself. George completely blocked the path, jammed between the brush, foliage, and trees. The Captain stared at him intensely, if not viciously, then came up with a strategic plan. He bent down, picked up one of George's feet, placed it carefully to one side as far as he could then picked up the other foot, spreading that leg also as far as possible. Now George was grumbling. Our leader stooped down and crawled between George's legs on his tip toes, carefully watching where he placed his feet. He successfully completed the passage, arose, and told George to turn around.

First we had to get his feet back in place on the path, then figure out how to have him perform a 180-degree turn. We had him raise himself on his tip toes, me in front, the Captain in back to help balance him. We both embraced him and had him turn slowly on his toes. He had to cross his legs so they would end up in the right places when turned around. He was not quite the ballet dancer as the Captain. We gingerly tracked our way out of the jungle, all three of us muttering, but not in harmony. We exited the path after which we were given orders to get in the plane, leave, and never come back. I assured him I would not. We took off, our honor guard not at attention. George was silent most of the way back to Guatemala City. I could only guess what he was thinking. We arrived at home base, and feeling guilty about the episode I had involved him in, offered him and he accepted $300 instead of the $225 we had initially agreed to. I had one more situation to check out before departing Guatemala. I had met a retired officer, Major Gustavo Giron, who was supposed to have a catch of Boeing P-26 parts. I had told him of my mission. He knew nothing of Curtiss Hawk P6-Es. He did have many P-26 parts. I located him and arranged a meeting to inspect what he had. He picked me up in a jeep and we drove some distance to a farm he owned. Adjacent to a house was a ten foot high concrete wall surrounding an area approximately fifty by fifty feet square.

As we entered the yard, I was quite surprised. In the center, laying on the ground was a partially crushed tail cone. It turned out to be the one I had tried to find. You can imagine my consternation. I had not thought to check with the Major before heading to the jungle. He had retrieved it some time previously and had brought it to his salvage yard. There were many tail feathers, landing gear assemblies, gas and oil tanks, fairings, and a few wings. He informed me that he had many, many more wings. I asked to see them. Another shock—he took me out to a large garden that was irrigated and, to retain water, was partially surrounded by a string of P-26 wings (I guessed possibly twenty of them) forming a dam.

After my inspection, the Major agreed to hold all P-26 parts for me. When I finished my South American tour, I would contact him and make arrangements to ship everything to the United States. It was time to move on.

Next stop: Lima, Peru.

CHAPTER SEVEN

Lima, Peru, and Emilio
(An Angel In Disguise, or
The Devil's Emissary)

The flight from Guatemala City to Lima, Peru, was uneventful. I made sure this time that I would be on a modern airliner, a Braniff jet. The flight arrived at noon. After landing, during taxiing to the ramp, I witnessed a strange sight. The one-story terminal building appeared to be about 200 feet square. There apparently had been a downpour of rain. On the roof was a bevy of men dressed in white coveralls, scurrying around with brooms, sweeping waterfalls of water off the roof. The building appeared to be fairly new, all marble and glass, but the inside was flooded with about a foot of water; another group of men with brooms were sweeping furiously to clear it out before the flight arrived. They didn't accomplish it. The passengers had to wade through the flooded lobby and custom aisles. I asked one of them who spoke English about this. He was nonchalant, said it happened all the time, and the white-clothed crew was always on hand because of frequent heavy rains. It seemed to me it would have been cheaper to repair the roof; however, this did create work for the natives. This was an incredibly poor country. Poverty was obvious everywhere.

After a lengthy period of time getting through customs—it would have been faster with a canoe—I managed to obtain a cab for the drive into the city of Lima. Along the route, I was shocked at the living conditions I saw. I had seen poverty and pitiful conditions in other countries, but this brought tears to my eyes. Along the road were partially built huts of mud and clay. Some had a few bricks stacked in front of them. The occupants would buy one when they could afford it and add to the small pile so someday they could replace the mud huts with bricks. That would probably never happen. Little children were standing or moving around, stark naked. I saw one bent down in front of a hut, expelling a bowel movement, another standing, his thumb in his mouth, urinating. There were no such things as toilet facilities or even out-houses. This sight continued for a long stretch into the city.

We arrived at the hotel that the airline had recommended. I satisfied my cab driver with a sum that seemed to please him to the extent he jumped out of the cab, unloaded my bags, and placed them on the sidewalk beside me, thanked me in Spanish and left. As I turned around, I was greeted by an excited voice. I am six feet tall. I completed my turn, expecting to be facing someone. No one there. Practically up against me about two feet below stood a little imp of an elderly man. "*Señor*, you weel need a guide. I weel be thee guide." I wonder how he knew that. I guess I looked pretty much U.S. American.

This was Emilio—Emilio Bobbio, who had been destined by fate to be my companion, advisor, military strategist, commando, banker, impersonator, and con artist during my stay in Lima. I must describe him.

Emilio was five feet tall, probably weighed 85 pounds. I guessed he was around 80 years old, but spry as a jackrabbit. His thin face was wrinkled, but lively and smiling. He was formally dressed as a chauffeur, a very proper gentleman. All the time he was with me, he wore a shiny black mohair suit that was way too big. The shoulders drooped over his tiny frame, the sleeves hung to his knuckles, the waist could encompass him once again, and his pants were overly baggy and piled up in wrinkles over his shoes. He always wore a white shirt—the collar four sizes too big—a string tie, and his too-small chauffeur's cap perched on top of his head. You couldn't help but love this little fellow. And you would never forget him.

Emilio spoke very little English, but enough to initiate some hot and heavy negotiating. His eyes closed to slits, his hands folded at his waist, his voice lowered to a cunning level, a whisper of a smile on his face, his head bent upwards and forward to lock eyes with me. I had to control myself from bursting out in laughter.

We discussed my intent as best I could with a mixture of Italian, Spanish, and sign language. When he understood sufficiently, we verbally mapped out a program and schedule. And that took some time; I was exhausted when we finished. I would need him for a period of three to five days depending how successful we were. Typically, Emilio asked for a daily fee three times too high, but settled for a fair cost. We agreed to start out at 8:00 A.M. each morning. It was mid-afternoon, I had phone calls to make. Before Emilio left, he informed me of one stipulation in our agreements: he was to handle the money. I would give him a daily sum to cover expenses. This was a good idea, for he could negotiate in Spanish and get better deals than I could.

After registering in the hotel, I contacted the U.S. Embassy for the phone number of a U.S. Air Mission officer, Colonel Christman. I reached him on the first call and explained the purpose of my visit. He knew nothing of old aircraft in the Lima area, only because he had not given it any consideration. He gave me a few ideas where I might look. He would be very busy the next few days and apologized for not being able to take time to escort me around the area. I told him that was not a problem; I had a guide. Oh Boy— He mentioned an aviation school ten miles north of the city. The Director of the School of Aero Technology was a Major Miguel De Lavega. I must see him at the airport for permission to enter the school and shops. I also had the name of a General Belascas, Director of Materials, who might know of the existence of any old aircraft.

Another possibility for information was a religious group, Summer Institute of Linguistics, under the direction of the Office of Ministry of Education. They would fly into the back country to teach religion. I contacted one of the group, hoping they might have happened upon crashed aircraft in the remote country. They had not. The first day in Lima had passed with no encouraging information.

At 6:00 the next morning, the phone jingled. I picked it up. On the other end was Emilio, down in the lobby, excitedly letting me know that it was time to begin our tour. I reminded him that we were to leave at 8:00 A.M. "No, no, *Señor* Raffael (as he called me) we mast go, we mast go. I weel wait for you over heere." I guessed he meant in front of the hotel. Not wanting to hold up my Commandant Emilio, I rushed myself together, grabbed a bite to eat in the restaurant, and headed for the lobby door. As I exited, I witnessed a sight to behold—right in front of the hotel door was parked a big black 1954 Cadillac limousine that sparkled like a jewel. I heard a voice coming from behind the automobile, a head popped up, Emilio. He was busy dusting the car, so I assumed it was his and my transportation during my stay in Lima. As I approached the vehicle, it reminded me of the DC-4 airliner I'd ridden from Mexico City to Guatemala. The Cadillac had as many dents and Emilio had them polished as shiny as the smooth panels of the car. What a match, the huge automobile and this tiny gremlin. (The dictionary describes a gremlin as a small creature humorously blamed for the faulty operation or disruption of any proceedure.) Whoever composed the dictionary must have known Emilio.

Emilio came around from the back of the limo and opened the rear door. I told him I would sit in front with him. "No no, *Señor* Raffael, you mast seet in thee bach. We mast have you to bee a verry *importanto* persona een Lima, Parru ahnd you mast drress up like I ahm." I was wearing slacks and a sport shirt—I had to go back to the room and put on a suit.

Emilio once again happily opened the back door, I got in, and he went around to the driver's seat. I saw the door open and close. I raised up to see where he was. He had just put on his chauffeur's cap, and that was all I could see of him from the back seat. He put a thick pillow under his rear. That raised him up so his head was just visible above the seatback. We were off in a screech of tires, and I tried to settle back with Emilio all the while carrying on a one-sided conversation.

I had prepared a three day outline for my search. I thought the first logical place was the airport to ask if anyone might have any information or rumors of old aircraft. Colonel Christman had suggested visiting the main operator on the field. I located him. He spoke good English; we talked for a period of time. Emilio had stayed with the limo to protect it. The gentleman was very accommodating, but knew of nothing. He had a couple of old cabin momoplane transports similar to a Beaver he jokingly offered to sell to me. I walked around the airport looking behind hangars and buildings, and at the far end of the airport behind an old shack, I found the remains of a Stinson L1B and some other unidentifiable parts of airplanes. Because of my pre-occupation with the Hawk, I once again passed up a rare find.

While at the airport, I tried to locate the Director of the Aero School of Technology to get permission to visit there next day. He had left. No one knew when he would return, so I decided to wait and spent the rest of the day talking to everyone on the field for any thread of information about old airplanes, but to no avail. And the Director did not show up. I was frustrated over this, but my Strategist assured me that it was not a problem. And he had a solution. The second day was over, no progress. Emilio dropped me off and informed me that he would retain my money because I did not know how to barter and would be giving too much away. My Banker. In our initial agreement, I offered him a bonus if he performed well. So the more he saved me, the bigger his bonus would be.

Next morning was a repeat of the previous one. At 6:00 A.M. sharp I got a wake-up call. Emilio. I gave up. The next two mornings I got up at 4:30 to be ready to go at 6:00 to appease him.

Emilio was waiting for me in the hotel lobby. As I approached, he had a look of disapproval. "No, no *Señor*, you mast drress weeth thee suit like me. Today, you mast be thee *Ministario de Educación*." I was wearing slacks, long sleeve shirt, and tie. Not good enough for a high ranking official. I went to the room and got my suit coat. Emilio was satisfied. He informed me it was a long drive to the school, ten miles, so we must leave early.

Now, instructions for my behavior when the time came to enter the School of Aviation. It would have required a special pass from the school Director we had not been able to locate the day before. To Emilio this was immaterial. I was to sit quietly in the back seat, "Act like a big Shot, but say nothing." Emilio would do all the talking. I was to be turned slightly towards him. If a guard would address me with a question, Emilio would nod his head slightly up or down if I was to say "*Si, si*" or left and right if I was to answer "No, no." If I was asked a question that required an explanation, Emilio would intercede.

And all this did happen. A heated discussion developed between my Advisor and the guard at the entrance gate to the school. Emilio excitedly and emphatically informed and reminded the guard repeatedly that I was the Minister of Education, my identity not questioned, and I should not be interrogated. My Commando (con artist) prevailed, and I began having visions of jail bars.

The guard opened the gate. As we drove through, another sight of wonderment—

This was a large outside combination work and storage area. On a number of wooden horses laid uncovered wings to be repaired. To the left, against a twenty foot high wall, 50 to 60 feet long, stacked like cord wood endways were dozens of bare Stearman fuselages. An equal number of tail feathers and wings were stacked in piles or leaning against the walls and fences. Engines, tanks, landing gears, and other parts were in a large shed at the corner of the yard. Incredible, but nothing I was interested in.

But—another of my notable goof-ups. My obsession for the Hawk had blinded me to other jewels. At one corner of the yard, unbelievably, was a complete little Twin Engine Hi-Wing Aronca—less engines—in reasonably good condition. I learned that only three had been built. Not rare enough, I guess—or just too possessed with the image of a Snow Owl on the side of a P6-E. I spent hours wandering around taking in this spectacle while Emilio kept the guard occupied and away from me. I don't think he was convinced of my identity. It was Saturday, the school not open, so I did not get to see any of the operation inside. Had it been a weekday, I would not have seen this anyway because of the danger of meeting someone who knew the Minister of Education. So Saturday was the right choice. By noon, I had finished surveying the yard. And was disappointed. The last two days I questioned many, many people who knew of no rumors of any type of old aircraft, not only in the Lima area, but also anywhere in the remote parts of the country. Even Major Giron in Guatemala, who had all the P-26 parts, suggested there might be some model or other of a Hawk in Peru. The school was the best possibility. The information I had received through the years about Peru seemed to have no credibility.

I walked to the limo and motioned to Emilio that we were leaving. The guard followed him to the car, all the while the two of them talking at the same time, neither of them stopping to hear what the other was saying. My Strategist at work. We drove out of the school yard to the highway for the long slow voyage to the city. He refused to abuse his Cadillac with speeds over 20 miles per hour. The original ten miles actually became 21 miles according to Emilio's calculations. He brought this to my attention two days later when we settled the cost of his services. A typical banker at work; more specifically, *My* Banker at work.

After lunch, we drove back to the airport. I wanted to make sure I had not missed any possibility. Through my Interpreter, a title I had failed to include earlier, we questioned practically everyone on the field. No luck. The only suggestion offered was the Peruvian Air Force Air Base which was on our agenda for the next day, my last one in Peru. A Colonel at the base had a Curtiss Osprey I hoped to see. By late afternoon we left the airport, and Emilio drove around to show me the city. One interesting sight was a huge outdoor market with hundreds of people scurrying around. He avoided the depressed areas, and we drove into a nice, clean, modern home development he seemed to be proud of. A little later I learned why. By 5:30 P.M., I suggested we return to the hotel so Emilio could be home in time for his supper. He lived with his married son, a Sergeant in the Peruvian Air Force. It immediately occurred to me that this would be our entry to the air base, through his son. Boy! was I wrong. Emilio, my Military Strategist, Commando, and Impersonator, had his own plan to infiltrate the air base which was restricted to only military personnel and government officials.

Instead of driving me to the hotel, Emilio informed me that he had made arrangements with his son and family to have me join them for supper. I accepted; it was a nice gesture. I guessed that he had told them about my reason for being in Peru. And from the reception I received when we arrived, he must have embellished my purpose and me to hero stature.

We had returned to the pleasant residential development we had driven through earlier and turned into the driveway adjacent to a very nice home. Emilio jumped out of the limo, opened the rear door, and as I stepped out, grabbed my arm and excitedly escorted me to the house. His son was expecting us and was waiting at the door. He warmly welcomed and thanked me for accepting the invitation to have dinner with them. A note I have, written by Emilio, shows his son's name as Lennico. He had been in the United States for military training. He and his wife spoke English clearly. As I recall, they had two children, and there was an elderly lady whom I guessed to be the mother of Lennico's wife.

Emilio was bouncing around introducing me to everyone, repeating a lengthy explanation of my mission to each of them individually. Lennico and his wife were watching with smiles on their faces. Half laughing, she asked how I was getting along with her father-in-law. I, too, was laughing and answered that he was "Something Else," but I was happy and lucky to have him as my guide. Knowing Emilio's methods, Lennico wondered if we had gotten into trouble yet. I answered: "Not yet, pretty close, but we still had one more day to go." He offered his help, but had to be on duty the next day and really couldn't do anything. Emilio had instructed me to say nothing of going to the base the next day. I always had to find out his thoughts and intentions the hard way. We spent a pleasant evening, after which Lennico drove me back to the hotel.

The next day was Sunday. Not wanting Emilio to be upset, I was on time, and in proper attire. I had no idea that it would be difficult to enter the Air Base, or that only military and Government Officials were permitted. Emilio was waiting for me in the lobby, rather than outside to protect the limo, to once again give me instructions for the day. My attitude and appearance when we approached the guards at the Air Base entrance was to be very aloof, arrogant, *and say nothing*. I asked why. "Because *Señor*, tooday, you mast bee thee *Ministario de Defensa.*" *Oh no—I could now feel and see those jail bars in front of me.* "Emilio. I can't do that. We both will be arrested for impersonating government officials." "No no, *Señor*, eet ees Sonday, no prooblem. I weel take carre of everrtheeng ahand my son ees oveer therr." Glumly, I reluctantly gave in and stumbled into the limo. After all, his son was on duty and maybe could bail us out of trouble.

As we neared the Air Base, several cars were lined up at the gate waiting for clearance to enter. Emilio got in line, honking his horn to establish our importance. An impatient guard approached and angrily told him to stop and wait his turn. Emilio would not let it go. He rattled off that we had to enter immediately, that we had an emergency situation. I understood enough Spanish to know what was going on. The guard ignored Emilio, turned, and went back to the front of the line. And I shrunk in size once again. I mumbled to Emilio to leave. He wouldn't. The gate entrance was wide enough for two cars side by side. Emilio pulled out of the line, sped through the gate past the other cars, the guard shouting at us, but unbelievably he let us go. Emilio had apparently convinced him of my identity. It was just a matter of waiting our turn, but had we waited our turn, we would have had to produce the necessary pass. This little con-artist knew all the angles.

Emilio pulled up to what appeared to be a headquarters building, parked the limo, and we got out. I did not know where he thought he was going. He headed for the hangar line; I followed. We didn't get very far. A guard stopped us, asked where we were going and what we were doing in the restricted area. Emilio told him we were going to the hangars to check on an aircraft for the government. Oh God. The guard refused to let us go any farther and said we needed clearance from headquarters to go out on the field. I whispered to Emilio: "*Vamanos.*" In English, let's get the hell out of here. "No no, *Señor Ministario*, wee weel geet thee pahss." I had no choice but to go along with the charade.

We entered the headquarters building and stood in the lobby as the guard went after someone to help us get a pass. Once again I whispered to Emilio for us to leave. To no avail. In a few minutes, an officer I guessed to be a Colonel approached us with a puzzled look on his face. Emilio started to explain why we were there. The Colonel cut him short, addressed me in English. He guessed I was an American and angrily demanded an explanation of why we were there. Just at that moment a Sergeant appeared down the hall, Emilio's son, Lennico. And he was mad as a hornet. The Colonel demanded to know how we got on the Air Base. I told him we drove through the entrance gate; the guard had let us through. I was looking for old airplanes, specifically a Curtiss Hawk P6-E. He did not know what a P6-E was, but there was a Curtiss Ospery on the field. I asked if I could see it and if it was for sale. Diverting him from his initial line of questions angered him more. He answered in no way could I go out on the field. I had trespassed on Government property, and an investigation would be necessary to determine how we got on the base in the first place. I had a vision of being incarcerated until the investigation would be completed.

At that point Sergeant Lennico intervened, informed the Colonel that Emilio was his father who had assumed it was permissible for him to be allowed on the base because his son was a non-com and Sergeant in the Air Force. The Colonel deliberated for a period that seemed hours, but was in fact a few minutes, left, came back and turned us over to the Sergeant with definite orders to get us off the base ASAP. I was ready. Sergeant Lennico escorted us to the limo, trying to control his anger at his father. Emilio was completely indifferent to the whole event and insisted we must go seek airplanes in the hangars. I wasn't the only Hardnose.

As we drove back to the city, I settled back, closed my eyes, and did some soul searching. In the first place, I began to doubt the existence of a Hawk anywhere in the world. And what was I doing getting myself into all these ridiculous situations? Emilio in front was chattering on and on about his disapproval of our treatment by the military.

We arrived at the hotel; it was middle of the afternoon, Sunday. I suggested to Emilio he should spend the rest of the day with his family. This way I would be assured of no more incidents or complications for the balance of the day. I wondered what kind of a reception he would receive when he got home. But then again, he was Emilio—there was no obstacle he could not overcome. My flight to La Paz, Bolivia, the next stop on my Safari, was to leave early the next morning, so we retained our 6:00 A.M. schedule. Emilio headed for home as unaffected as usual by the events of the day. Before leaving for the airport the next morning, I settled with Emilio. He took the initiative, determining hours, mileage, meals, inconveniences (I wondered if he meant to him or me), and stand-by periods. All this was written down in English, I guessed by a family member. His final figure was somewhat higher than the original estimate. I paid him what he asked for plus a nice bonus. It was worth it to be free and alive. He was happy as a lark, gave me his address and phone number in Lima in case I visited again. All the way to the airport Emilio carried on his usual one-sided conversation. A mental image of this little fellow would be embedded in my mind the rest of my life. Shortly thereafter I boarded a Braniff Airliner and was on my way to La Paz, Bolivia.

CHAPTER EIGHT
La Paz, Bolivia

The elevation of the airport at La Paz is approximately 13,000 feet. A flight attendant informed us before landing not to walk too fast after deplaning. The air was very thin at this altitude, and one could become short of breath. I guess I wasn't listening as well as I should have been. I exited the plane door, down the steps to the ground, and started to walk briskly towards the small terminal building at the top of a rather long stairway. Within a short distance I began puffing, slowed down, started to ascend the steps, stopping several times for air. So were the other few passengers who deplaned. I slowly got to the top, entered the terminal, and leaned on a counter to rest and catch my breath. A young boy approached me; he appeared to be seven or eight years old. "*Señor*, Coke A Cola?" I was ready for one. I asked how much. "One dollar, *Señor*." He had that same cunning look in his little eyes. Uh uh—a miniature clone of Emilio developing. Cokes were not that expensive in 1970, even a long way from home. I accepted his charge, gave him a dollar—which he grabbed—and ran off like a fox. All the passengers who got off the plane were natives and had rides waiting for them. I was left alone, no taxis at the terminal as one would expect. I found a telephone and managed to order one. It was an hour before it showed up. I told the driver I wanted to go to the *Hotel Crillon*. When we left the terminal, I was the only one in the cab. That was to change several times on the way into town.

La Paz is surrounded by mountains that form a huge crater. The city sets in the bottom at an altitude of 5,000 feet. From the airport at 13,000 feet to the level of the city, a narrow road winds down around the inside of the bowl. It is a long, slow, nervous drive, constantly going in a huge circle. Above the road, built on sides of the hills and mountains are homes and shelters that follow the road to the bottom of the crater. Anyone wanting to travel to a lower level, or down to the city from where they live, must have some form of transportation—an automobile, taxi, horse and wagon, horse or mule. Well, I provided transportation for a large number of natives moving from top to bottom, or from one level to another, in my community taxicab.

We had driven a short distance from the airport when we saw a man waving the cab down. The driver stopped, they talked a few seconds, the fellow got in. That was OK with me; now someone would share the fare. A little farther down the road, two more men, driver stopped, few words, they got in. Boy, this was going to be almost a free ride. Another short distance, this time a woman, few words, she got in. Now there were six people in the cab, four in back, driver and one in front. Down around the bowl a ways, another pick-up, four in back, three in front. Now I am starting to get worried.

About halfway down to the city, the driver stopped, let two riders off. But I saw no fare paid. Soon the lady was let off, no fare paid. There were still four paying passengers left, so I could hope. We continued on. Another pick-up, this time a Nun. This was OK. I needed some religious support. Another stop, all got out but the Nun. But, no fare paid by any of them. I tried to carry on a conversation with the Nun. I guessed that she did not want to talk. At the edge of the city, near a church, she spoke a few words to the driver, he responding graciously, "No, no." I knew what that meant: free ride. I wouldn't have objected to that anyway; at least she was the only one who offered.

We were well into the city. The driver had slowed down. As we approached what appeared to be the main business district, he stopped. I cringed at the sight in front of us. There were hundreds of college age young men, some on foot, others in pickup trucks. They were shouting, yelling, waving arms vigorously, and carrying many, many signs that read: "Damn Yankees," "Hate Yankees,""No Yankees," and other descriptive phrases. Occasionally I heard gunshots. What in the Hell was I doing here (a phrase I often repeated on this Safari)? No doubt they could spot me as a Yankee. I shrank down in the seat (I had a lot of previous practice doing this), jerked off my tie, opened my collar, and tried to look as Latin as I could. I hoped being Italian would help. In fact, during my stay in Bolivia, I told everyone I *was* Italian. But they all knew I was a Yankee.

It was after 4:00 P.M.; the demonstration began breaking up. I could see the sign of my hotel just a few blocks away. My driver carefully skirted the demonstrators and inched around to the front, let me off, and I paid the fare without question, an amount that certainly included the free riders. I just wanted to get in the hotel and out of sight.

As soon as I was settled in a hotel room, not wanting to loose any more time than necessary, I contacted the officer in charge of the U.S.

Military Group in Bolivia, Colonel Charles Reed. I briefly explained my mission, after which he suggested I come to his office. It was around the corner from the hotel and up a few steep blocks. The day was turning into dusk. He advised me to hurry before dark. There were a few snipers in the area taking pot shots at almost anyone. I left the hotel, and as I practically ran up the hill to the office, I heard several gun shots (once again that repetitive statement).

Colonel Reed introduced me to two U.S. Officers also stationed in Bolivia. We spent an hour discussing my purpose for being there. They knew of older aircraft in the country, but nothing of a Curtiss Hawk P6-E. After we ended the meeting, Colonel Reed offered to spend the next day with me and show me around the Bolivian Air Force Air Base. There were a few aircraft I might be interested in. He drove me to the hotel and suggested I have dinner at a Chinese restaurant directly across the street to avoid wandering around to find a place to eat and exposing myself to sniper gunfire. At that time, Bolivians did not like U.S. Americans, and it was obvious that I was one.

The Bolivian Air Base was located at the same airport used by commercial airlines. To get there required that long slow corkscrew drive up the side of the crater bowl to the 13,000-foot elevation. We stopped at the entrance gate to the Air Base for clearance to pass through. This took a few minutes. To one side of the gate was parked a complete P-47 American-built fighter plane on static display. I gazed at it nonchalantly, believe it or not, disinterested in such a jewel, blinded only with visions of a Curtiss Hawk P6-E. Many years later, when visiting the Champlain Fighter Museum in Phoenix, Arizona, Doug Champlain was showing me the collection of fighter aircraft. As we walked down the row of World War II planes, I stopped in front of a P-47. I stood looking at it and told Doug of the one I had seen years earlier in Bolivia, but had made no effort to purchase. He smiled and informed me that this was the same one. He had acquired it by an even trade for one of his planes.

We soon had clearance to enter the Air Base. We drove ahead for a short distance. In front of us, another sight to behold: Perched on top of a twenty-foot-high concrete pedestal was a Curtiss Wright Falcon CW-R19, an all metal low wing airplane used as a fighter in earlier years. This was the one with the fixed landing gear and wrap-around wheel pants fairings. This was a jewel; I now got excited. Because it was a permanent display, I assumed it could not be purchased. I remarked to Colonel Reed that I was extremely interested in the airplane, would buy it if possible. He thought it might be for sale, no harm finding out, and suggested I meet and get to know some of the Bolivian officers, then bring up the subject. I got around to that the next day.

We arrived at the headquarters building where I met the Commanding General, Fernando Sattori, and several other Bolivian Air Force officers. They were all very courteous, congenial, and accommodating. General Sattori gave us permission to explore the Air Base at our leisure.

Behind a shed in a salvage yard were three large metal wings, less fabric. No one knew what make of airplane they had been on. There was a complete radial engine on a mount, a skeleton fuselage of a Stinson, piles of crashed airplane wreckage, a covered Stearman fuselage, and a complete Stearman in fair shape. Setting in an open space some distance from the junkyard was another sight that excited me: two Curtiss SNC-1s that had been moved to the salvage area. One was complete, the other less wheels, propeller, and some engine cowling sections. I was sure these could be purchased, since they appeared to have been discarded. I would offer to buy them the next day at the same time as the Falcon on the pedestal.

The day passed too quickly with all these exciting finds. It was late afternoon. Colonel Reed had planned for me to have dinner with him and his wife at their home. Certainly very gracious and considerate of them. I am sure he didn't want me wandering around, a sniper target. He dropped me off at the hotel so I could freshen up and picked me up an hour later. We spent a pleasant evening during which I explained in more detail my mission. From La Paz, the next stop of my journey would be Cochabamba, then on to Santa Cruz where the Curtiss Hawk P6-E was supposed to be, the high point of my Safari. Colonel Reed knew of a Staggerwing Beech owned by a retired Bolivian Major who was operating a flying service at Santa Cruz. He had known about the plane for some time and hoped to acquire it before he left Bolivia, asked me to find out if it was for sale. With me, it was a Curtiss Hawk P6-E; his obsession was a Staggerwing Beech.

I would need a charter or rental plane to fly to Santa Cruz and Cochabamba. Colonel Reed said this was not a problem. The Bolivian Air Force could rent me a plane and pilot. It seems they needed every source of income to subsidize the Air Force due to limited funds provided by the government. That also could be the reason they might consider selling the Curtiss Falcon on the pedestal.

Colonel Reed made arrangements for me to meet with General Sattori, Commander of the Bolivian Air Force, the next morning. A U.S. officer came along as interpreter. At the headquarters building, I was escorted to the General's office and waited in an outer room until he had time to see me. The room was dark and completely bare of furniture except for the single chair I sat on. Standing in each corner of the room were four small men dressed in black civilian suits, white shirts, black ties, and black hats. I could only guess that they were Secret Service Agents or guards. I don't think they liked Yankees; for more than the one hour I waited, they stood glaring at me unflinchingly. Reminded me of my experience at the jungle airstrip at Guatemala, except these fellows didn't have machine guns or hand grenades hanging from their shoulders.

My interpreter, who had been in the General's office all this time, motioned me to come in. I felt relieved to leave that dark waiting room. The General was friendly and congenial. He spoke acceptable English, but for extensive conversation he talked in Spanish with the interpreter. He asked the purpose of my visit. I told him I was interested in purchasing the Curtiss Falcon R-19 on the pedestal at the gate. He answered: "*Señor*, in Bolivia we will sell anything. What is your offer." I had a number in mind, thought for a second, having had previous experience negotiating with Latins, and threw out a figure half of what I originally intended. Amazingly, he accepted. I gave him a check for the agreed amount. We shook hands and discussed making arrangements to ship the aircraft to the U.S.A. I then asked if I could also buy the two Curtiss SNC-1s in the salvage yard. He deliberated for a moment, but decided that they would keep them for aircraft mechanics training. Next point of discussion was my need for a rental plane and pilot for several days to fly around Bolivia. That was not a problem. It was early in the day, about 9:00 A.M. I asked if arrangements could be made to leave by noon. The first stop would be Cochabamba, only a 150-mile flight. That was not a problem, so we planned for a 1:00 P.M. departure. I returned to the hotel to pick up clothing and needs for a three-day trip, leaving the bulk of my baggage behind, since the next leg of my Safari to Columbia would originate from La Paz.

Colonel Charles Reed and Bolivian Air Force officers.

Curtiss Wright CW-R19 (above and on next page).

CHAPTER NINE

Flight to Cochabamba:
The Captain and the Crew Chief

I arrived back at the Air Base early, 12:00 noon. The day was clear, the sun blistering hot. I was dressed lightly, wearing thin summer-weight slacks and jersey. I was allowed to roam around the hangars and wondered what type of aircraft would be assigned for the cross country trip. There was none out on the line except a 180 Cessna. I dismissed it as the plane to be used since it appeared to be in need of substantial repair. Again, it reminded me of that DC-4 airliner I had ridden from Mexico City to Guatemala City.

Our scheduled departure of 1:00 P.M. came and passed; no plane or pilot. 2:00 P.M., no one. The heat was overbearing. I was perspiring profusely, every few minutes wiping my forehead to keep the water out of my eyes. Finally at 3:00 P.M., I saw two military personnel approaching, one an officer, the other an enlisted man. I was trying to dry my brow to stop the flood and froze with my handkerchief on my head at the sight before me.

It had to be a mirage. The officer, a captain, was dressed in full winter dress uniform including leather gloves. The enlisted man was a sergeant, also in winter olive drab full dress uniform. Both were sweating as much as me, but cheerful and ready to fly into the wild blue yonder. I was very privileged to be honored with all this formality. The captain introduced himself. He was Captain David Velasques, my pilot. The Sergeant was a crew chief. I didn't know we needed one, but I was soon to understand.

I asked why they were dressed in full uniform in this hot weather. The Captain answered that this was an official flight and required formal dress. Then I inquired of the airplane for the flight. The Sergeant pointed towards the Cessna 180 parked a short distance away. As I stared at it, I mumbled, and a few choice thoughts passed through my mind (another habit I seemed to repeat too frequently during this Safari). I asked if this was the only plane available and remarked that it did not seem to be in very good condition. The Captain stated that this was the charter and cross country aircraft they always used. And the Sergeant politely and emphatically informed me that it was in very good condition because he was the crew chief of this particular airplane.

I was relieved to notice neither the Captain nor the Sergeant had luggage (I had a small bag). At the airport altitude of 13,000 feet we should be as light as possible for take-off. I guessed we were ready to board, opened the cabin door to enter. There was no back seat, just a canvas sling to sit in, probably removable to carry cargo or eliminate weight. I climbed in and sank into the miniature hammock, certainly not very comfortable. The Captain got in, followed by the Sergeant, no pre-flight performed. I asked about this, but was assured that it wasn't necessary. Was the oil checked? Not necessary.

With everyone in place, it was time to start the engine. I leaned forward to watch procedure. The instrument panel was far from cosmetic and matched the interior of the airplane very well. The Captain and Sergeant were excitedly talking back and forth, the Sergeant giving instructions. Priming seemed excessive to me, the throttle completely closed, engine cranked, loaded up, and would not fire. This went on, with throttle closed time after time, the crew up front arguing how to get it started. Several times I suggested they leave the switch off, throttle wide open, turn engine, and let it clear out. They completely ignored me. The Sergeant would turn to me frequently: "Very soon, *Señor*, very soon we go."

In exasperation I asked the Captain to let me start it, but the Sergeant assured me that they would get it running. Finally the throttle was pushed wide open. The engine cleared out and sputtered to life. "We go, *Señor*, we go." I scanned the instruments. The oil pressure gauge was not indicating, the needle on zero. I shouted to the Captain to bring this to his attention. "No problem *Señor*." Suddenly the Sergeant began banging on the top of the instrument panel, causing the needle to jump up and down. "See, *Señor*, we have the pressure." He continued hammering. The gauge fluctuated, started to stabilize and indicate some pressure. "*Señor*, is OK, we go, we go." With that assurance, but with my apprehensions, we began to taxi out to the runway.

The journey to the end of the runway was a revelation in taxiing to me. I had always throttled my engine to a steady RPM to maintain a nice comfortable speed. I learned a new technique this day. One must intermittently operate the engine from idle to high RPM to move the plane in spurts, this method being demonstrated very efficiently, plus the jerking kept me alert. All during taxiing, the Sergeant proudly proclaimed: "*Señor*, we go to Cochabamba, we go, we go to Cochabamba." These expressions of confidence were very reassuring. It was stifling in the cabin, but my flight crew seemed oblivious to the heat and were talking back and forth constantly. I couldn't help noticing the gloves the Captain was wearing, I suppose to soak up the perspiration in the palm of his hands to better manage the controls.

We turned onto the runway for take-off. Once again I was reminded of our destination and: "We will go now." There was no seat-belt in back, so I firmly grasped whatever I could on the sides of the fuselage. The hammock seat would sway with the motions of the airplane; I didn't feel too secure. There seemed to be an air of apprehension up front. I tapped the Captain on his back to get his attention, told him I would love to fly the airplane. Before he answered, the Sergeant interrupted: "No, no, *Señor*. The Captain will fly us to Cochabamba. He is good pilot. We will go."With that, he turned around and started beating on the instrument panel, and triumphantly exclaimed: "We go."

The take-off procedure was very similar to the taxiing technique. I was learning to fly all over again. Full throttle was advanced to get the plane rolling, retracted, advanced, retracted, and finally left in full advance halfway down the runway. All the while, the plane was fishtailing left and right and hippity-hopping, bouncing up and down trying to get airborne. This of course was due to the high altitude. I was flopping around in the hammock, again mumbling through gritted teeth those familiar phrases that came involuntarily. On one final bounce the plane took to the air in a blaze of glory, still fishtailing.

The climb out of this high elevation airport was slow, shallow, and laborious. About 15 minutes after departure, I was puzzled about the direction of our course. The crew up front was having an aggressive conversation when the Sergeant began pointing in various directions, the Captain disagreeing. I leaned forward, asked if there was a problem. The Sergeant apparently was our navigator, answered; no problem, we were on our way to Cochabomba. I became suspicious. I had a map of South America, Bolivia in the center, showing our destination. It was a clear day, and I could see some landmarks. I looked at the compass: it indicated that we were going straight south. Cochabomba is east of La Paz. I shouted at the crew, asked where their map was. They had none. I informed them that they were going in the wrong direction. They accepted my information without question or argument. I gave them a compass heading which they turned to, thanked and praised me for the guidance. I sat back, tried to relax. Unbeknown to me, my lips began to quiver, and I heard sounds of a familiar nature coming out of my mouth.

Now that we were on course, I closed my eyes for about twenty minutes, opening one eye frequently to check the compass heading. My head was cocked to the right. I decided to open both eyes. Looking out the side window, the sky was clear, visibility unlimited. Below was a beautiful valley between the mountain ranges, several thousand feet lower than our flight altitude. I casually turned my head to look out the left side window. I jerked up in the hammock, my eyes flipping wide open. The air had been more than moderately rough. Now I knew why. We were barely skimming the mountain tops bordering the valley to the right, bouncing and flying in and out of powder puff clouds over the mountains. The airplane wheels were just clearing the peaks; I could have reached out and touched them. I shouted to the Captain, asked why we were flying this path when a short distance to the right was wide open clear air over the valley. He answered that this was the shortest route to Cochabamba; we would save time. I insisted we veer to the right. He refused. Now my vocal emissions were not unpremeditated. It was another 30 minutes to our destination. I could only hope we would get there without further incident. Guess again.

Another uncomfortable 20 minutes passed. We broke out of the now scattered clouds at the end of the mountains. Ahead I saw Cochabamba. To the south of the city was the airport that appeared to have a combination dirt and hard-top runway and a wooden control tower. The plane was not equipped with radio equipment, and clearance to land was not necessary. After we passed the mountains, the Captain began a diving descent towards the airport. As we neared it, he did not enter a pattern, but continued the dive right at the tower. I sat up in alarm as he dropped to tower level, gave wide open throttle, and performed a 360-degree vertical turn no more than fifty feet away and a hundred feet above the ground. I could clearly see the tower attendant's face as he waved a joyful greeting to us.

The approach to land was at full throttle up to about one-half mile from the airport. Then began World War I procedure. The throttle was pumped in and out all the way down to the ground. There was a dirt and gravel pad at the end of the runway. We hit it at excessive speed, bounced, fishtailed, and leap-frogged most of the way down the runway. We came to a stop, the Sergeant exalting over the accomplishment of the flight and performance, addressed me: "*Señor*, The Captain is a good pilot, no? He is the best pilot in all of Bolivia." We taxied to a parking area; I fell out of the airplane. Captain Velasques was a good-natured fellow; he laughed and remarked that the landing was not too good. He was happy-go-lucky, spoke good English, and we became good friends. He liked to party, and that we did.

With the delay getting started to leave La Paz and the extended flight route, we arrived at Cochabamba close to 6:00 P.M., too late in the day to began a search. Captain David would stay at the base. He borrowed a Jeep, drove me into town. I registered in at the *Gran Hotel*. The building was square, two stories high, a large open-roof courtyard in the center with tables for dining and social gatherings. We had dinner together and a few *cervezas* that put the Captain in a party mood. I reminded him that we had a busy next day, no time for partying, and turned in for the night.

I planned on only one day in Cochabamba, not expecting to find anything of any consequence. We searched the airport, found nothing. This was not a vary active civilian or military base. The Sergeant (our Crew Chief) knew the area, obtained a Jeep, and now became our guide and chauffeur. Most of the day we drove to remote areas, asked many natives if they knew of any old aircraft. Nothing. We returned to the hotel right at dark. Another disappointing day, but Captain Dave reminded me: "Tonight we will have good time." And boy, did he.

We started out with *cervezas*, not bothering to eat. After a few, he gathered up practically everyone in the courtyard, mostly girls, invited them to our long picnic-type table. By now everybody is calling me: "Yankee *Gringo*," all of us singing, me partly in Spanish, partly Italian, didn't make any difference. Then came the champagne. By 10:00 P.M., Captain Dave was sailing high. I was ready for bed, but no, we had to go to another cabaret. He was out of money; I gave him enough to last the night and sent him on his way. I navigated to my room and flopped on a cot that was the bed, thinking of home.

Santa Cruz, the next leg of my journey, was 200 miles east of Cochabamba. This was the crucial and most credible possibility of my entire Safari. I was hoping to leave early, but should have known better. I had no idea when Captain Dave would show up. I checked the military barracks, but he had not returned to the base during the night. I learned that the Cabaret he went to was more than a drinking establishment and guessed he had become entrapped by a bevy of *señoritas*, the occupants. He had.

I don't know why, but there was a spot of grass under the wing of the

Cessna. I lay down, my bag under my head to wait patiently: it was 9:00 A.M. Shortly after noon, I saw someone approaching. It was Captain Dave, looking as if he had been run over by a tank. He had a sheepish but happy look on his face. "*Gringo*, you have missed a good party." It was hard to get mad at this guy. I resignedly asked if he was ready to leave for Santa Cruz. "No, *Gringo*. The weather is not good." I looked to the sky, clear as a bell. There were a few powder puff clouds over the mountains to the distant west, in the opposite direction we were going. Also, he stated that we had lost our Sergeant and could not leave without a Crew Chief. "Don't worry, *Gringo*, we will leave tomorrow," after which he turned and weaved his way to the barracks. I spent the rest of the day retracing the previous tour of the airport and asking questions with no results.

CHAPTER TEN

Santa Cruz: Dissolution of a Myth and End of a Saga

Captain Dave had fully recovered from his self-appointed holiday celebration, in shape to ascend into the sky above. We no longer had a Crew Chief, so I sat up front as co-pilot and navigator. Also, it was my duty to beat on the instrument panel to activate the oil pressure gage. We negotiated the usual take-off procedure and leaped off the runway. I discreetly suggested our flight direction, determined from the map of the whole of South America. No other maps were available. This route placed us over open space and valleys, away from mountains. Our departure from Cochabamba was early. We arrived in Santa Cruz at 11:00 A.M., in time to arrange to seek out the ranch where the Hawk was supposed to be. This was the number one priority.

By noon, I found a driver and Jeep to take me into the remote area where the ranch was located. Captain Dave had relatives in Santa Cruz and would visit them until I returned. To save me time while I was gone, he would check the airport for the possibility of any old aircraft.

The information I had placed the ranch fifty miles north of Santa Cruz. The first twenty-five miles was paved road, the remainder dirt. With all the disappointments throughout my Safari, I was not as excited as I might have been. Along the winding dirt road were a few natives working in the fields. They knew of the landing strip and exact location of the ranch. It turned out to be a small farm, and there was a field that had once been an airstrip, overgrown with brush. There was a barn not too far from a hut in which an elderly couple lived. They confirmed that the Air Force general had lived there; they had worked for him many years, but knew nothing of an airplane. I walked to the shed, entered with apprehension that turned into disappointment and a degree of anger. Had I been led on a wild goose chase by someone with a twisted sense of humor? Feeling thoroughly disgusted, I vowed that this was the end of my Safari.

But it was not the end of my problems in Bolivia.

CHAPTER ELEVEN

Flight to Nowhere

Returning to Santa Cruz was a silent, thoughtful trip. I decided to cancel all further travel in South America—or anywhere in the world. I had to assume that there was no Curtiss Hawk P6-E in existence except the mock-up at the Air Force Museum at Dayton, Ohio. My only concern at this point was to return home, re-evaluate the entire situation, and make a final decision either to give up or build the Hawk. With original factory plans, I could produce the real airplane. I had the tool and die facility and the manpower to build a P6-E.

I hoped to leave for La Paz as soon as possible, change my itinerary, and return to the U.S.A. Captain Dave was in the city; I did not know where to contact him. I could only hope he would be at the airport early the next morning.

It was noon when he showed up. He said the weather was bad along the route; if it did clear, it would be too late to get to La Paz before dark. I spent the rest of the day talking to military personnel and civilians, inquiring about any knowledge of old aircraft. Nothing.

Mid-morning next day Captain Dave informed me that the weather was still bad; we could not leave. It was clear as far as I could see in every direction except, again, a few puffs of clouds over the distant mountains. He left, and I was getting impatient to leave. I decided to call Colonel Reed to get weather conditions in La Paz. He informed me that the weather was perfect and had been for several days. My pilot must have had some other reason for delaying our departure.

I decided to find another plane and pilot. There were two flying services at the airport; one of them agreed to fly me to La Paz in a Cessna 180. I suggested we leave as soon as possible so that the pilot could drop me off and return before dark. He was Bolivian, spoke some English, said he was very familiar with the route. Once again, no maps. I still had my map of South America.

We took off at 11:00 A.M. A direct flight path would take us straight to Cochabamba and La Paz with a flight time of a little over three hours. The pilot took up a northwest heading; I thought we should be going westerly. When I brought this to his attention, he answered that this was a short cut. I disagreed, but he was the pilot navigator. As we progressed, we penetrated deeper and deeper into solid, dense jungle country. Had we taken a straight west heading, we would have followed the single paved road leading to Cochabamba. We were almost two hours into the flight when I noticed that the pilot seemed to show signs of uneasiness. This made me nervous. I asked if there was a problem. No answer. "Are you lost?" I asked. He was not sure, but I was. If this kept up we were going to have a fuel problem.

The jungle was solid in every direction as far as I could see—and becoming frightening. Then one of those things that kept happening to me all my life materialized again. Just ahead, on the ground, unbelievably, I saw a swath cut in the jungle. It was an emergency landing strip one of the oil companies had constructed. I told the pilot to land. He willingly agreed. The strip was not very long, so I told him to come in slow and just clear the trees. His approach was too fast, too high. I pulled the throttle, dumped the flaps he had forgotten, slowed the airplane and dropped it in. The end of the strip was coming up fast, I shouted for him to slam on the brakes and cut the switch. We skidded to a stop on the grass about twenty feet in front of a solid wall of jungle. I sat back in the seat, eyes closed, and angrily reprimanded the pilot. He sheepishly admitted that he had gotten lost and did not know where he was. On this big map of the whole country, I showed him where we were; by calculating time and speed I had determined that we were 100 miles off course.

I started to climb out of the airplane, had the door half open—and froze. *Not again.* Out of the jungle, on both sides of the grass strip, came groups of natives bearing those long knives that look like curved swords.

My God, head hunters? I thought. *When is all this going to end? Maybe too soon.*

I got out. The pilot got out. We stood waiting for what, I didn't know. The natives had stopped a short distance from the airplane and were just staring at us. I hoped they thought we were Gods who had dropped in on them from the heavens, which in fact, we had.

One of them slowly approached. I wondered which of us was first choice. He started to speak in Spanish, assuming, I suppose, that we would understand. My pilot answered. They were gathering edibles from the jungle and were not hostile. Thank God we were not edibles. Or were we? Most of the natives returned to the jungle. A few stayed, sat on the ground, and watched until we left.

I determined that we had enough gas to return safely to Santa Cruz before we reached the point of no return to anywhere. My pilot was ready to agree to anything I suggested. He was apprehensive about taking off. I told him I would fly the airplane. He said he was responsible for it and could not let me. I assured him I would help from the passenger seat if needed. It was mid-afternoon and *hot*; lift would not be too good. We taxied to the absolute end of the strip, lined up, held back, gave full throttle, released brakes, and started rolling. Didn't look too good. As we picked up speed, the trees were coming at us fast. I called for him to begin lift-off and instantly dumped the flaps. We staggered into the air, barely clearing the treetops. I held the wheel to prevent him from trying to pull up. We skimmed along over the trees to pick up speed, gained some altitude, and I slowly retracted the flaps. I gave him a heading, made sure he held it. We got back to Santa Cruz without incident. But did he get *hell* from his boss. There was no charge for the flight.

Another day lost. Captain Dave nowhere to be found. My only alternative was to take the airliner that stopped at Santa Cruz once a week; I had no choice but to wait three days before its arrival. After what happened those next three days, I should have walked to La Paz.

CHAPTER TWELVE

Hostage

To pass the time for three days in a small, remote town in the center of South America I thought would be boring. Not so. Before the end of the first day, without warning, my short stay was to become considerably more exciting.

Now, I thought, would be a good time to look for the Staggerwing Beech airplane for Colonel Reed of the U.S. Air Mission at La Paz. The civilian flying services were at the opposite side of the airport from the military installation. As I recall, there were two or three hangars. The Staggerwing was in the first one I walked into. It was in excellent condition, had been well cared for. While I stood looking at it, a gentleman came out of the hangar office. He was a retired Bolivian Air Force Major. The airplane belonged to him, was not for sale. He knew Colonel Reed.

Typical of South American military officers, the Major was a gentlemen, congenial and courteous. We spent a few hours talking, he telling me of his background and I telling him of my mission. He knew of no vintage airplanes other than his Staggerwing and the ones at the Air Base in La Paz. I told him of my flight the previous day. He had heard about it, that the pilot had gotten lost and was 100 miles off course. Then the Major made an observation I tried discretely to agree with. He commented: "*Señor*, the Bolivian pilots do not fly very well." I carefully answered that I agreed with him and described a few of the experiences flying from La Paz to Cochabamba and Santa Cruz with an Air Force Captain.

The Major became silent. The pleasant look on his face turned to one of anger. He turned away and strode back to the office. I didn't give it much thought until I heard him talking vigorously on the telephone. I stood by the door listening. I knew enough Spanish to understand some of what he was saying. He described me as an assassin, spy, secret agent, and more. I walked into the office, perplexed, wondering what I had done, the Major glaring at me.

After he finished the call, I asked him what was wrong, what had I done. He angrily instructed me to sit down. He refused to talk or answer my questions, *and* I could not leave. The time was about 2:00, middle of the afternoon. I sat silent for an hour. Then, another repeat performance. Here they came. Six little men in black suits, white shirts, thin neckties, black hats—and a mean looking leader dressed the same. They surrounded me still sitting on the chair. The leader demanded my passport and wallet, all the while the Major glaring at me. Two of the gentlemen grabbed my arms, lifted me out of the chair, and escorted me to a black limousine. All seven got into the limo, jammed in on each side and in front of me to make sure I couldn't escape. And once again, those mean, never-wavering, piercing eyes.

Each time I started to ask the leader what this was all about, I was told to remain silent. They drove to the motel where I was staying. The leader led me into the room, informed me that I was under guard until the airliner came through in two days, and I was to leave the country immediately. I asked for permission to call the American Embassy. He refused, left, locked the door, and placed four permanent guards outside around the clock. One of them brought me food, but I was not permitted to leave the room the next two and one half days.

The time came to leave. I was driven to the airport, all of us jammed into the limo. The leader arranged my airline ticket. After all the regular passengers were boarded, the squad escorted me to the airliner. The leader gave me my passport and ticket and warned me never to come back to Bolivia. If I did, I would not leave alive. One last time I demanded to know what I had done. He glared at me: "You know what you have done in this country. I do not have to tell you. You know what you have done." The only possible reason could have been my agreeing with the Major on his comment that Bolivian pilots were not too good, and I unwittingly described the lack of skill of a Captain David Velasques. I found out later: *his nephew.*

The Safari was over. I refused to continue the search in Central or South America any further. I'd had it. I re-routed my flight to shorten the trip and get home as soon as possible. Arriving at Miami, Florida, the first thing I did was find a concession stand, gulp down a quart of milk, a hot dog, and thank God for the good old U.S.A. Then I continued on to Omaha ASAP.

CHAPTER THIRTEEN
Initiating the Dream

In early 1969, I planned a major business expansion program and purchased a 200,000 square foot building. Preparing it required extensive remodeling, with completion scheduled for March, 1970. I had planned my Hawk Safari during that period so that when I returned we would move the plant from the previous 22,500 square foot building to the new location. The new building was one and one half stories high with a third level at the front for administrative staff and show rooms. The sub basement or lower level was 100,000 square feet of warehouse space. In one corner, I had a special room constructed for building the Hawk. It was completely secured; no one was permitted to enter except those of us actually working on the plane. Throughout the years, most of the 200 employees never knew what was going on in that private room.

Returning from South America, I was discouraged and upset with the results of the trip. I had to concentrate on moving and prepare for the substantial increase in business, but I could not postpone or let the Dream fade and die. I had 35 tool and die makers, the manufacturing equipment, and the facility in which to build the airplane. Also, I had original Curtiss Hawk P6-E blueprints, Curtiss Conqueror engines and manuals, stacks of information, and an original wing from airplane #32-260—but no one other than myself qualified to build the airplane.

I had taken my Stearman to Cliff DuCharme's shop at West Bend, Wisconsin, for an annual inspection in 1969. Ray Goss usually worked on the airplane. During that visit, I offered Ray the opportunity to move to Omaha and help build the Hawk. I would not have much time to work on it; running the company was first priority to earn the income to afford to build the ship. Ray considered the offer, but was reluctant to leave West Bend.

By early 1971, I hadn't found anyone. Then a real stroke of luck. A friend knew of a German aircraft metal and master mechanic, Herb Tischler. I located him, flew to Tampa, Florida, and met with him. He had worked on and built airplanes in Germany, moved to Ecuador, South America, to modify helicopters, then back to Tampa to repair aircraft. We discussed building the Hawk. Shortly thereafter, he and his family moved to Omaha, and we initiated an outline of procedure to build the airplane.

At this stage, I must state that research, development and construction of the Hawk would normally be the focal point of the story. But actual building of the airplane became incidental to events that developed causing delays, postponement, and possible termination of the project. Through the years, many thought the Hawk P6-E project was a myth, thought it probably never existed. Also, rumors persisted that I had passed away. I will, however, offer a brief explanation of how a few of the more difficult parts were made, then describe the horror stories that ensued. Having been in a job shop and contract manufacturing operation it was normal to assign work orders for all parts to be made. I wanted an accurate record of hours of labor performed to build the Hawk. The first step was to make hundreds of individual drawings, from the factory blueprints and microfilm, of every piece of the airplane to distribute to the toolmakers for machining. Special gussets and brackets for the fuselage were being made while Herb built the frame jig. All materials—such as tubing, sheet metal, bolts, and screws—were as specified on original parts lists. We brought an expert welder from Florida to do all the welding, both steel and aluminum. Herb built the fuselage and hand-made all the aluminum sheet panels which we sent to Lindberg in Chicago for proper heat treatment and temper. The most difficult items to manufacture were the landing gear struts. They could have been fabricated out of sections of tubing, welded, machined, and ground to give the correct appearance. I would not make them this way; they had to be original. One half inch thick wall 4140 steel tubing cut to proper length was set up in a lathe, the inside diameter taper bored and honed with special stones to remove tool machining marks. The outside diameter was taper-machined and polish-finished. The lower end had to be radius bent without collapsing the tubing and would require special equipment. No one in the country would make this bend and guarantee the outcome. The solution was to make a number of one quarter inch thick washers mounted on a shaft and machined to the taper of the inside diameter of the tubing at the bend area. These were strung on a cable and dropped into the struts, then shipped to Chicago to a tube bending company that still would not guarantee the results. I told them to go ahead anyway; we had no choice but to try. We got the struts back; they were not collapsed. Herb and I looked at each other to decide who was going to try to knock the shims out. We expected them to be locked in place. Herb used a long rod, tapped the end gently to get a feel for how tight they might be jammed. Miraculously, the washers slid out.

The second most difficult item to build was the radiator. I had two built by specialty shops; neither met my standards. Herb, with his matter-of-fact outlook on obstacles, casually said he would build it. He did, and it came out beautifully. We had to make form dies for some of the parts, the rest Herb hand-made.

The wings were built by woodworking specialist Arnold Nieman of Milan, Michigan. A few antiquers suggested the trailing edges be made of curved wood inserts between ribs to eliminate the chance of wrinkles if cable was used. I refused to do this, and did end up with a few wrinkles, but it is as the originals. I have a wing to prove it. We used the steel fittings and brackets from the original wing, so there would be a few original P6-E parts in the airplane. Herb installed the aluminum leading edge panels and wiring.

One major stumbling block was finding a propeller. I didn't think this would be a problem. Surely, somewhere in the country I could find one. After fifteen years of traveling and searching, I gave up and ordered a block of alloy steel to manufacture the hub. As a result of my ads in *Trade-A-Plane*, an elderly gentleman in Florida called a few days after the steel arrived. He had a hub of proper specifications and would sell it for $350. That same day, I put one of my men on an airliner to Florida with a cashier's check. To have machined a hub out of a solid block of steel would have cost a small fortune. Next, the problem of the blades. Here again, I had not found any over the fifteen year period, so decided to have a set machined. I located four oversize blades with the proper shank specifications and shipped them along with the hub to Miami Propeller Service. They machined them to proper size and shape, mounted them into the hub, and shipped the complete prop back to Omaha.

The Curtiss Conqueror engines and parts we shipped to Steward-Davis, Inc.—an airplane engine rebuild and repair company in Long Beach, California—with instructions to do whatever was necessary to build one complete direct drive engine. We were fortunate to have two new cylinder banks to be used on the final unit. All accessory items were to be rebuilt to new condition specifications.

There are many aluminum castings in the P6-E. The cost of patterns was prohibitive. I had toolmakers machine parts out of blocks of the proper spec materials. When completed, we glass-beaded them to give the appearance of castings. The only item not textured was the tail wheel fork; that, we polished.

All the instruments in the airplane are original type. It took several years to locate and procure the complete set, one or two at a time. Oddly enough, we found most of them in Canada, then sent them to an instrument shop for reconditioning. The radio inside the cockpit is the old coffee grinder type. There is no modern navigation equipment in the airplane, only an original compass. I came from the road map era and can get anywhere without compass or navigation aids. I want the P6-E to be completely original.

There is not much of a landing gear shock system, only a small hydraulic cylinder mounted to each strut with 1³/₈" travel. Landing shock is absorbed by the underinflated tires, pressure-set at 20 instead of 24 lbs. This gives them a flattened appearance on the ground.

The 600 HP Curtiss Conqueror V-1570CM engine is liquid cooled using pure Ethelyne Glycol as cooling agent and operates at virtually no pressure. A small amount of water in the system is dangerous, can turn to steam and cause an explosion. The cockpit is completely lined with aluminum sheet metal to protect the pilot should this happen. The Glycol must be changed frequently to prevent deterioration of the product, resulting in a highly caustic reaction injurious to the engine. The engine is bolted solidly to the engine mount; there are no rubber or shock pads of any kind. Surprisingly, there is practically no vibration when the engine is running.

By the middle of 1972, Herb had the fuselage well along, including some cowling and metal work. I had four toolmakers working full time for the past year and many, many parts were finished.

My business was growing rapidly. I was involved in many phases of manufacturing, not only job shop, but my own product line. I was producing a complete line of recreational vehicles, hundreds of thousands of mini bikes, go-carts, three wheelers, utility trucks, and mini-bicycles. The move into the larger facility had paid off. Company sales increased from $1,000,000 to $4,500,000 in two years. The building, equipment, and total facility was capable of producing an ultimate volume up to $25,000,000. This was my goal in a seven year program being planned with major manufacturers in the automotive and related industries.

To grow this rapidly would require periodic injections of substantial equity capital. With the plan in place and $2,000,000 of initial contracts in hand, I began to seek funds to implement the program. I could not go to banks; I did not want to borrow money or create debt. I needed investors.

I contacted an investment group in Iowa. They were extremely interested in working with me. After two weeks of negotiations, we came to an agreement, and on a particular Friday afternoon I received a phone call informing me of their unofficial decision to go with the plan. They were to have a board meeting the following Wednesday, after which I would receive the official decision. The first stage of the agreement required an injection of $300,000 when closing the deal. This amount and the normal cash flow would support the company for the period necessary to set up a complete administrative staff; $500,000 would be provided every six months thereafter. As product was shipped and accounts receivables grew, additional funds would be needed progressively to support growth up to the point the company became self-supporting.

I informed the source of the contracts that Friday afternoon of the situation. They were pressing me to start producing as soon as possible. I had not committed to or signed contracts as yet. I didn't dare until the agreement with the investors was consummated. Then the events of the next few days changed my life forever and affected the progression and continuation of the Hawk. As stated at the beginning of this story, "My erroneous choice of associates in business."

Next 14 pages show various stages of construction of my Hawk P6-E.

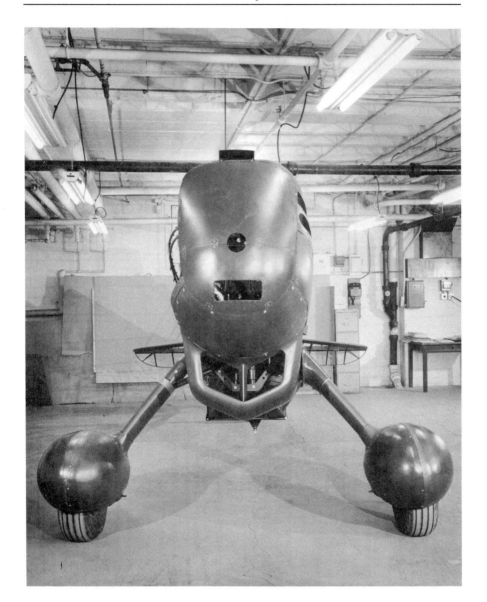

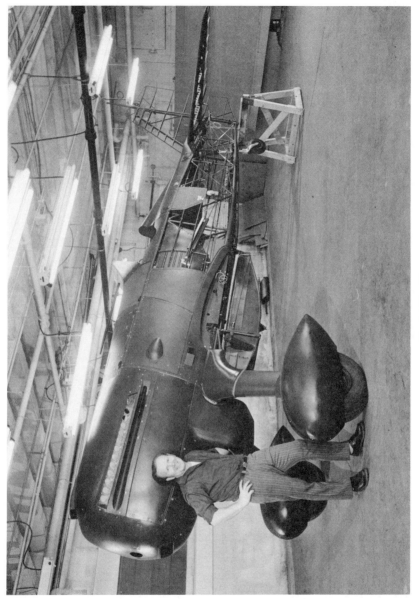

Herb Tischler

Herb Tischler and Larry Jensen

Herb, Larry, and me.

My original wing off P6-E #32-260

Larry Jensen

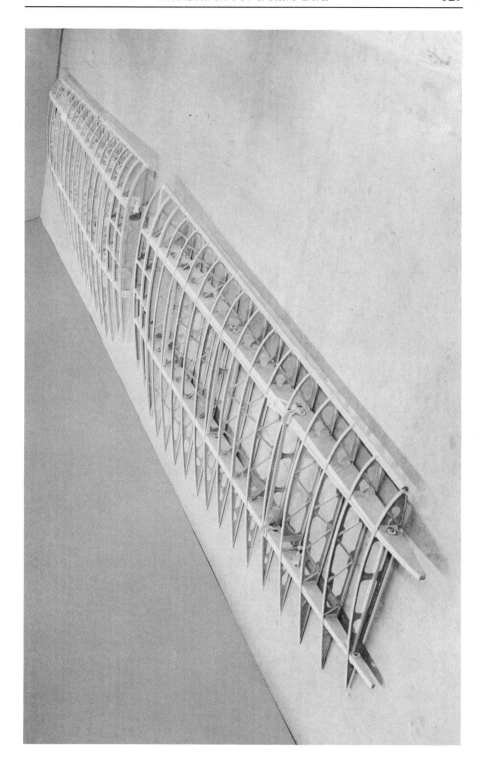

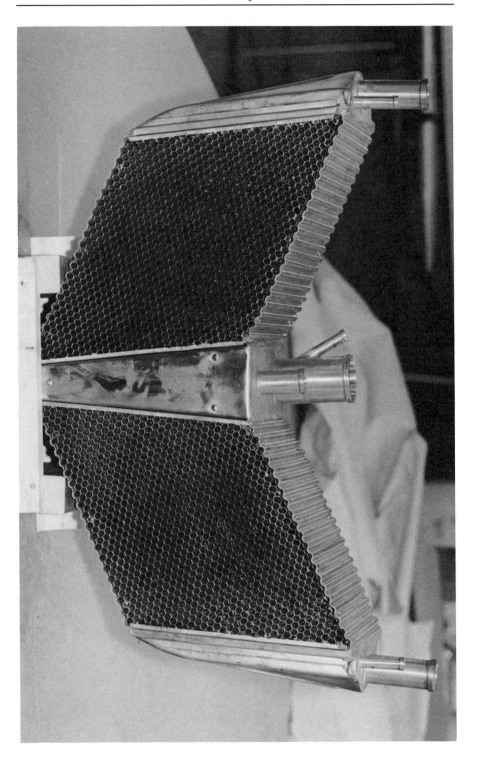

CHAPTER FOURTEEN

Black Sunday:
The Beginning of a Never Ending End

It would be five days before I got the official decision from the investment group. It was a Saturday morning. I began to plan setting up an administrative staff to grow with the new company program. I had run the $4,500,000 volume operation myself with only three employees in the office.

Mid-morning, I received a phone call from a local retired business entrepreneur. He had heard of the program of growth and suggested we discuss his possible participation. I arranged to meet him at the plant the next day, Sunday morning.

He had never been in my plant. He was astounded when he saw all the machinery, equipment, and production lines. He immediately understood that it would be no problem producing five times the volume in the facility. I then took him up to the third floor showroom; he was elated at what he saw. He remarked that he had not seen this quality of merchandise anywhere. Then came his reason for the meeting. Having been in business all his life, he knew that to grow as fast as I was planning, there would be a capital problem. He had grown so fast in his own business, cash flow had not kept up; he'd almost lost it. His only salvation was to sell stock, which he reluctantly did, but realized many millions of dollars. Shortly after going on the market, he sold the company, took substantial stock as part of the sale price, then dumped it, which made a lot of people mad.

He was excited about my situation. He suggested we work out an arrangement whereby he would invest whatever amount was needed, no limit. I informed him that I was working with an investment group and would have official confirmation of our agreement in four days, Wednesday. I would require $300,000 on closing, then $500,000 in six months before accepting new contracts. I had orders on hand in the amount of $2,000,000 along with the normal flow of $4,500,000. These were the terms accepted by the Iowa investment group. Additional funds would be required periodically until cash flow caught up, and the company became self-supporting.

That was not a problem for him. He had funds available (he said). Why wait until Wednesday. Go with him. We could shake hands on it right then. I would still run the company. One stipulation: the next election year, after the company reached a level of $20,000,000, I had to agree to go public. He had done well before, going on the market, and apparently wanted to do it again with my company.

Early Monday morning, I telephoned the contact person I had been working with the past year structuring the new program. He represented the source of the contracts, and I had to keep him informed of financial progress on a daily basis. Time was critical; we had to get into production as soon as possible. I told him of the development of a new investor—identifying him by name—who claimed to have the financial resources to support the program and would commit immediately, then suggested we meet the next day to confirm his offer.

Present at the meeting on July 25, 1973, was The Investor's business manager, Orville McIntosch. They already knew the basic outline of the program, so we got to the point. We had to know right then if the potential investor could support the projected growth, and we needed financial statements to substantiate his offer. He said he would provide them (he never did), but it would take several days. We reviewed the program. It required progressive injections of $500,000 of equity capital every six months for possibly a period of two years or more. The Investor was completely casual and matter-of-fact and stated that this was not a problem. His business manager was silent throughout the entire discussion. The meeting ended; handshakes confirmed the agreement. We had no concrete confirmation from the Iowa group, so we concluded that we should go with the new Investor; "A bird in the hand is better than two in the bush." Another classic quote. The next day I met with The Investor's manager, McIntosch, at their bank. I needed to have the $300,000 payment in hand before I called the Iowa group to stop any further activity with them. I called my attorney before I deposited the check in the company account. No documents had been prepared; it would be a few days before either attorney would have them ready. The handshakes and verbal agreements would stand as a legal binder. I was apprehensive about his opinion, but deposited the check on his advise. I contacted the Iowa group and informed them of the decision to go with the local investor. That, in effect, closed the door to any future re-consideration from them. I state that for a reason.

A month passed when I got a call from The Investor's attorney requesting that I come to his office. He had talked to my attorney, and there seemed to be questions about the agreements. I met with him; he presented me with documents and notes concerning the $300,000 advance. The agreement he had prepared—but had not submitted to my attorney for review—set out that I was to give up my voting rights, an option for The Investor to acquire 51% of the stock, his business manager would take over running the company, and I would be reduced to shop operations only. The advance was in the form of a loan to the company instead of equity capital, and I was to personally guarantee it. I was stunned at all these changes. The attorney then questioned the amounts of future funds that The Investor was to contribute to the company. I told him that he had offered whatever it took to bring the company to the ultimate level agreed to by everyone at the meeting. The attorney repeated: "*Any* amount?" I responded that he had, and after the meeting he had dictated a letter stating his intentions and what he agreed to. The attorney seemed to be taken aback. He suggested that I take the documents and review them with my attorney. I had endorsed the $300,000 check with the company stamp and personal signature as instructed by my attorney. I could feel the screws beginning to turn. And it was a long, long screw that twisted for years. There is more than one way to interpret that phrase.

The meeting with my attorney was a drawn-out affair. He had known of the entire situation from the beginning, but had wanted to review the agreements. He had many conversations with The Investor's attorney, and it was a month before he called me in to arrive at a solution. I offered a counter agreement. They could purchase up to 49% of the stock at current value, funds he provided must not be loans but equity capital, I would still run the company, and I would not give up my voting rights. All that went down the drain quickly. The only stipulation he agreed to was purchasing the stock at current value and acquiring only 49% of the stock whenever he decided to exercise his option. He still had control if I gave up my voting proxy. My attorney's opinion was; if The Investor was going to supply capital to the extent he agreed to, he should have complete control. I was in a corner; I had nowhere to go. I had lost the Iowa investment group, deposited the $300,000 in the company account, and was hiring administrative personnel—and being pressed to start production on the new contracts or be in default.

While all this was going on, Herb had the Hawk fuselage, tail feathers, and most of the sheet metal finished; the wings were ready to cover, but the engine was still in California. He had reached a stopping point, did not profess to be a fabric man, and without the engine there was no more he could do. He had reason to go to South America and left Omaha in July, 1973. Larry Jensen had started a short time before Herb left. He was an excellent metal, fabric, and engine specialist and was on the project almost three years, until late 1975.

In August of 1973, the engine was finished and ready to be picked up at Steward-Davis in Long Beach. They had it loaded in a rental truck on the test stand; I did not want to take any chances having it shipped to Omaha. My wife Angie and I flew to California and drove the truck home.

During the three years Larry worked on the Hawk, he installed the engine and everything related to it, covered the wings, tail feathers, and fuselage. His wife worked with him throughout the entire three years, his son part time, and a few EAA members occasionally helped.

CHAPTER FIFTEEN

Embezzlement

After the financing agreements with The Investor were finalized in September of 1973, I was reduced to production operations. McIntosch took over as plant manager. He had no knowledge of this type of manufacturing and depended on me to guide him. He took over selecting the administrative staff and went overboard setting the company up as if it were a giant corporation. He had complete control of finances, but hired a high-priced CPA to manage company accounting, costing, payroll, and expenditures. He was another person who knew nothing about manufacturing or production costing. Then, one of the biggest mistakes McIntosch made against my advice.

When I developed my own product line a few years earlier, I had hired a marketing and sales manager. He had nationwide contacts and generated substantial sales. McIntosch elevated him to Vice President of Marketing and put him in the position to handle financial matters along with sales, accounts receivables, and, of course, to keep his own records of all these activities. One of his very important duties at the end of each month was to provide the controller with the inventory of everything in the plant.

The Sales Manager knew of the new injection of capital. He had developed an appearance of stress and anxiety the past year that seemed to become more intense. I was concerned. He explained that he was having problems with his two young boys. I accepted his reason; however, he became relaxed, and his usual pleasant outlook returned as soon as the new funds had been provided, and he knew more were coming.

He was big, weighed about 275 pounds, in his forties, baby-faced, congenial; everybody liked him. And a terrific salesman. He also enjoyed the good life. As time passed, his mode of dress improved. He had developed a private social life that did not include his family and had became very private. He appeared to be a devoted family man and had a nice home. I did notice, the last time my wife and I visited them, that the home had been completely remodeled and refurnished with all new furniture. I was paying him well, but I did wonder how he could do all this so quickly.

While out of town on a three-day business trip—I personally called on all major accounts periodically—I received a call from my secretary. She suggested I get back to Omaha as quickly as possible, but did not want to explain on the telephone. I canceled the rest of my trip and returned the same day.

My secretary had intercepted a phone call from Indiana for The Sales Manager. He and his secretary had been out of the office at the time. The party was a customer. He wanted to know if the three truck-loads of merchandise had been shipped. My secretary said she would check with our shipping department and let him know. I would normally screen all orders before processing, then turn them over to be put into the system. This particular order had not been channeled to me. It amounted to approximately $65,000. I called the customer with the excuse that I needed the order number to trace the shipment. He had placed the order by telephone a month earlier with The Sales Manager, who a few days later flew to Indiana on the pretense of calling on customers in that area. He had suggested that if the customer would give him a check for the full amount, he would allow a substantial discount; furthermore, postal delivery where the plant was located was unreliable and mail many times had been lost.

The three truckloads had left a few days earlier. I asked the shipping manager where the bill of ladings and other documents were. He would normally turn them in to the office for billing. The trucks had been loaded at night, and he'd had no knowledge of it. Since the Sales Manager was in charge of taking inventory, the items on the shipment were still shown in stock. With millions of dollars of product in the warehouse, it was not a problem to cover the discrepancy. I contacted the truck line to stop delivery. It was too late. The customer had received the three truckloads late the day he had called. He had paid for the merchandise; there was nothing I could do. The Sales Manager had deposited the check in his personal account. He had done nothing illegal by endorsing the check. He was an officer of the company. But, stealing the merchandise was another matter.

I decided to investigate more deeply into the situation before informing McIntosch. Within a matter of days, a similar operation occurred. Late one Friday evening, a rental truck backed up to the loading dock. The shipping clerk was just leaving. The Sales Manager was at the dock; he informed the clerk that he had an order from Montgomery Ward in Lincoln, Nebraska, that had to be delivered early the next morning, Saturday. The clerk was puzzled; Montgomery Ward usually picked up with their own trucks. He questioned why the rental truck and was told that Ward's trucks were unavailable; they'd had to rent one. Also, the paperwork would be taken care of, and the truck was loaded with $16,000 of merchandise.

Saturday morning, the shipping manager told me of the activity the night before. I called Ward in Lincoln and talked to the store manager; he had not placed an order with us. The truck was a Hertz rental. I called them, and they confirmed that a truck had been rented in Lincoln and returned before noon Saturday. I called accounts in Lincoln and found where the load had gone. The owner acknowledged receiving the merchandise, was elated over the 50% reduction in cost, and gave The Sales Manager a check for $8,000 on the spot.

I then called McIntosch at home, told him what had happened. Monday morning I instructed The Sales Manager that we were to be at the attorney's office early that afternoon. I invited him to lunch, after which we went to the meeting. When we entered the office, he looked frightened and nervous. Present in the room were McIntosch, the company accountant, and a detective. The attorney informed the Sales Manager of the purpose of the meeting. The Sales Manager dropped his head, started crying, (a maneuver he used frequently at court hearings), and admitted the thefts and embezzlement. When asked to what extent, he professed not to know, and I am sure he didn't. He was arrested, but released on bail.

A few days later I obtained a court order to have his checking and savings accounts released, and I personally reviewed them. And what a shock. In a fifteen month period he had embezzled approximately $500,000. Most of it had been spent in cocktail and Go-Go lounges. Checks written to sixteen different dancers and girl bartenders in amounts up to $1,000. He had set his number one Go-Go dancer up in an expensive west Omaha apartment with all new furniture, paid all her expenses, rent, clothing, and provided her with an automobile. He spent up to $500 a day in Omaha's top Go-Go Club. When I questioned the owner, I learned that he assumed I must have been paying the employee extremely well.

Three weeks after he was arrested, I got a phone call from his number one girlfriend. She insisted I meet with her. I was puzzled, wondered what she wanted, so I decided to go. Her apartment was large and beautifully furnished. She remarked that she had something I might be interested in, went to a closet and carried out a large salesman suitcase. She opened it. I was amazed at the contents. The suitcase was jammed full of shipping tickets, bills of ladings, customer purchase orders, hand-written invoices, correspondence, and canceled bank checks and statements. It was hard to understand why an embezzler would keep every bit of evidence that would incriminate him and then assume he could trust his girlfriend with all this information.

She was angry at him. He had told her The New Investor was going to provide hundreds of thousands of dollars to the company, and there would be no problem acquiring money whenever he needed it. He had not paid her rent for two months, and she would be evicted when the third payment was due. Additionally, she lost the car, and he had not covered her living expenses and was avoiding her. She offered to sell me the evidence for several thousand dollars. I told her I already had all the information I needed to convict him and offered her $500, which she accepted.

With all the evidence I had accumulated, the embezzler was found guilty as he sat in the courtroom crying. The Judge, affected by this sorrowful scene, released him on four months probation—no restitution—then two weeks later reduced the probation to three weeks. The man went free. The next three successive small companies he worked for went bankrupt as a result of embezzlement. None of them pressed charges, and he is a free man today. I was so enraged at these results, I reported the situation to the Internal Revenue Service to have him audited for income tax evasion. I received a letter from them stating that the case did not warrant investigation. Unbelievable. The Investor was upset over the situation, blamed and reprimanded McIntosch, removed him from the company, and put me back in charge. A short time later, McIntosch warned me to be careful. The Investor was working towards assuming ownership of the company, the building, and was maneuvering to get the Hawk. Six months later, McIntosch died of a stroke.

CHAPTER SIXTEEN
More Turmoil

In spite of the embezzlement problem, the company was still self-supporting. McIntosch had hired fifteen employees for the administrative staff, which was starting to eat heavily into the cost of operation. I accumulated $3,500,000 in new contracts. Six months had gone by from the time of the agreement for the first $500,000 to be provided by February 1, 1974. I contacted The Investor; he assured me that it was not a problem. A month passed; no word from him. My source of contracts in Chicago was upset and pressing me to get into production. Without the new funds, it was impossible. The Investor had left the country, was in Mexico. I called him; he assured me that he would be back in a few days and make arrangements for the funds.

I called Chicago, gave them the information. They, in turn, instructed me to come in for a meeting. I was put on the carpet; they demanded to know where The Investor was. They tried to contact him in Mexico, but he was not available. While I sat in their office, they prepared a final letter giving him ten days to perform on the agreement or they would terminate all contracts. I hand-delivered the letter to his office in Omaha. His secretary located him in Mexico; he told her that he would be in Omaha the next day.

I was in his office the next afternoon when he called Chicago. The letter they had written was strong, definite, and final. He once again assured them that he would have the funds to me within twenty-four hours. Then, in my presence, he dictated a letter to them confirming the phone conversation and commitment. I had not signed the contracts as yet and told him that I would not until the funds were in the bank. No problem. I kept hearing those famous last words all my life. I was to pick him up at his home the next morning. We were to go to his bank to make arrangements for the funds. When I arrived, he was dressed in bib overalls, no shoes, bare feet, and was trimming flowers in his front yard. He informed me that he was too busy to go to the bank; he would call me in a few days for another appointment. I reminded him of the urgency of the situation. That didn't bother him.

We did finally go to his bank a week later, still within the ten days.

He had $3,000,000 in municipal bonds, but they were all encumbered with many loans he had made on failed ventures. The bank declined to advance him any more funds. He had implied throughout our relationship that he was worth $100,000,000. Later, his banker provided me with a financial statement showing a net worth of $11,000,000, *but* of no consequence in the United States—practically all of it was based on properties in Mexico.

During the week before we went to the bank, I decided to lay the groundwork with another large bank. I met with the president, whom I knew, and explained our needs. He knew The Investor well and would supply up to $1,500,000 in a combination of cash and credit. We met with the second banker, who would provide us the financing but had to have $2,000,000 in bonds as security. The Investor declined, but did not explain why. Later, I privately told the banker. After this second meeting, The Investor stated that there was nothing more he could do, and I would have to seek financing.

I chased all over the country with no luck. The Investor had hired another business manager, a high finance man, but he could do nothing. I held Chicago off until the first of June, 1974. They refused to wait any longer and canceled several million dollars worth of contracts. From February to June, 1974—while waiting for the new capital—the controller and McIntosch, assuming the funds would soon be in the bank, ran the company checkbook $220,000 overdrawn, and most of the checks released. The controller was frantic, could not take the pressure, quit, and disappeared (more about that later). He had tried time after time to make The Investor understand how serious the situation was getting, but to no avail. I took the checkbook away from both the controller and McIntosch. It took me two months to get it covered.

Then, yet another blow. The controller, for the first two quarters of the year, had not made federal witholding and social security tax deposits. He did not even file the reports required by federal law. I discovered this when I saw the returns laying on his desk after he had disappeared. This amounted to $100,400. McIntosch had been discharged, so it became my problem; I was president. The Internal Revenue Service could not find the controller, so they came after me. I had to pay it out of my wages over a period of two years.

Another problem was created by the purchasing agent. Under McIntosch's direction, he ordered $300,000 worth of gasoline engines. I had advised them not to place the order until money was in the bank. With the contracts canceled, we had a warehouse full of engines I had to dispose of. And take a beating.

It was up to me to restructure the company. The Investor walked away, said I could handle it. His new business manager tried to find financing. He couldn't, gave up, and he walked away. I dismissed the entire administrative staff except for two of the women who had been with me for years and knew what it was all about. From 200 employees, I reduced down to 50. The job shop portion of the company always had been self supporting, both tool and die and contract manufacturing. From June to October, 1974, I stabilized the company and brought it to a profitable level. During this period, about two weeks before he died, McIntosch visited me often, repeatedly warning me of The Investor's intentions to take the building and the Hawk, which was approximately 75% finished.

Another outrageous situation was developing during 1974 and into late 1975. A local manufacturing company was buying three-wheel vehicles in truckload quantities from me. This continued for a time, then suddenly they stopped ordering. There was a broad market for the product, and they knew it; they had tooled up for a similar unit while buying my product. This came to light in August of 1975. I received a call from the head cashier of the bank in Omaha with which I was doing business. The bank provided me financing for inventory, equipment, and accounts receivables. The Cashier came to my office in a state of anxiety. He had been forced to supply information to one of the owners of the manufacturing company, who was also chairman of the board of the bank. Under the threat of loosing his job, the Cashier was instructed to furnish the Board Chairman with a list of my accounts and volume of business I did with each one. The Cashier eventually told the president of the bank, who called me for a meeting. He remarked that he was very upset with the chairman of the board of the bank and suggested I file a lawsuit for fraud and conspiracy against the bank, the Chairman of The Board, and his manufacturing company. He and the bank would back me up. I met with my attorney to determine a course of action.

With all the adverse events never ending and McIntosch's many warnings, I decided in August of 1975 to move the Hawk. The timing was right. Had I waited another month, I might have lost it. I sorrowfully informed Larry Jensen that we had to move the airplane unfinished. The engine was installed, wings, tail, and fuselage covered and in partial color. Larry had assembled the airplane completely in the shop, made the "N" and Cabane struts, fitted the flying and landing wires, then disassembled it to be moved. He did one hell of a job.

We packed everything related to the airplane, then had to figure how to get it out of the sub-basement of the building. The move was premature; I had not planned for it, so I had to do something in a hurry. This was developing into an emergency. I hired a demolition crew to blast a hole in the two-foot-thick concrete wall of the building and build a ramp up to the ground level. To this day, the few of those present at that operation still shake their heads. Everyone always wondered how I was going to get it out of the building.

The next step was to determine where to store it. I had no idea for how long. I was not too concerned in the beginning about actually hiding it; I just wanted it out of the building. The most immediate storage place I could think of was a "T" hangar at the airport. That's where we took it, but not for long—the spys were out.

CHAPTER SEVENTEEN

Shattered Dreams

Friday, September 2, 1975, 3:00 P.M. An officer of the Bank, followed by a deputy sheriff, entered my private office. The deputy handed me a court order closing the plant. In shock, I demanded to know why. I was not delinquent on loans. The bank was well secured, three to one ratio collateral to debt; I was their biggest account, and they did not extend me the courtesy of a meeting to inform me of their intentions. I was outraged.

Looking out the window, I saw four cruiser cars in front of the building—why, I could not imagine. I told the banker I would go with him to the bank immediately and meet with the president, who a week earlier had advised me to sue them and the chairman of the board. First, I called a meeting of all the employees, told them what was happening and to check with me the following Monday. Thank God, I had moved the Hawk; it would have been locked in the building for the next two years.

I called The Investor to inform him of what had happened. Even though I had been running the company after McIntosch died, he still had control, and I was responsible to him. He was completely indifferent, told me to handle it as best I could, then resigned as chairman of the board of my company and did nothing to protect his interest.

The bank said that they'd closed the company because they had agreed to provided interim financing *only* until The Investor had fulfilled his commitment. He hadn't. They did not trust him and were concerned that he would liquidate assets. I didn't think the explanation justified their action. I would learn the real reason in a few days; they intended to sell at auction the machinery and inventory to satisfy debt owed them. I contacted The Investor's attorney, who put the company in Chapter 11 of the Bankruptcy Code to stop the bank action.

There were two definite reasons the bank took the action to close the company. One of my past employees somehow learned of the possibility of a lawsuit against the bank, the Chairman of the Bank Board, and his company. The employee practically rushed to tell the Bank Chairman what was ensuing. Then, a second past employee gave more false information about the situation. The Bank Chairman called a special meeting of the bank board, instructed them to shut down my company, then left town. At one time, the second employee had been a close friend. We had worked together. I'd taught him the tool and die trade.

He had committed an unforgivable act. He had worked for me twenty years, most of the time as tool and die supervisor. Once when I was out of town on a business trip, he had been drinking and went to my home on the pretense of checking to see if my wife Angie was all right. She was alone and allowed him in the house. He continued to drink at the bar in the family room, then made improper advances toward her. She did not tell me for three weeks. I was outraged, rushed to the plant and physically ejected him. Going to the Board Chairman was his act of revenge to get even with me, although he knew that he was wrong and asked for my forgiveness several times. And the Bank Chairman, to show his gratitude, arranged with the bank to provide him capital to set up his own tool and die company.

The next two years—September, 1975, through October, 1977—were living hell. When the bank closed the plant, they froze all cash in the company account. I couldn't take care of accounts payable, not even utilities. I was alone in the huge 200,000 square foot building—electricity, gas, water and telephone shut off, no sanitary facilities. Only one person, my quality control manager, stuck with me. We could work only during daylight hours. Using a telephone in the library down the street, we kept in touch with creditors, banks, and attorneys. Forget about "friends." They all deserted me, not that I would ask anything of them. How quickly you are forgotten. You become bitter and angry. But, That's Life.

By the end of September, 1975, I had formulated a plan of reorganization under the Chapter 11 code. The Investor still had control until the plan might be approved, which took two years. I had to submit it to him for approval before filing with the court. He had no idea what it was all about, but gave me authority to do whatever was necessary to carry it through to confirmation.

Before the plan could be approved, many functions had to be completed. All frozen funds would be applied to bank debt. Inventories of finished product, engines, hardware, tires, plus most of the machine tools and production machines and equipment went on the auction block for a fraction of market cost—$3,500,000 of goods went for less than $500,000. As a result of The Investor's failure to provide the financing he had agreed to, all inventories were encumbered by loans from three banks. Advances on product contracts and accounts receivables were pledged. Raw materials unpaid for went for pennies on the dollar. Under the plan I submitted, I asked to retain enough machinery to start a new business that would generate income to satisfy the balance of negotiated debt.

After almost two years of working to dispose of everything in the building, the balance of bank and supplier debt was approximately $3,000,000. Banks would not settle for less than what was due them. Suppliers settled for various percentages of amounts owed them. Internal Revenue and State Department of Revenue were first priority. The net settlement was $2,500,000.

The inventory and product bank financing was guaranteed by myself and The Investor. He filed a claim for $1,220,000 to be paid to the banks to cover that debt through him. Had the company continued, it would have been self-liquidating.

It was a massive undertaking, but I knew I could do it if I could find financing *and* if I was left alone. Confirmation of the plan was set, oddly enough, for August 11, 1977, my birthday. I wouldn't call it a birthday present. Then The Investor raised his ugly head. He refused to agree to the plan unless I titled the building over to him. In addition, he wanted another $250,000—or the Hawk. He had a buyer for the building for $1,300,000, which would have satisfied his claim. I countered with $75,000. His attorney informed him of some of my comments, after which he agreed. The plan was confirmed, and I had to start all over at age 59.

Knowing I was going to lose the building, I had been looking for one in the same area. Real estate was much cheaper in this part of town. I found a 22,000 square foot building, borrowed $100,000 to buy and remodel it. With two helpers, I moved the machinery I was allowed to keep. In October of 1977 I began operations. Under my plan of reorganization I did not have to make payments for six months, except to The Investor. I was to pay him $1,000 per month starting January 1, 1978. This would be hard to do. I was broke, had no operating capital.

I went to every bank in Omaha, but was turned down. One in particular will always stick in my mind: The First National Bank of Omaha. I made an appointment with a commercial loan officer, a young lady. I presented my program and the amount of funds I was seeking. She was busy playing with her fingernails, occasionally looked at me, then asked how old I was. I told her 59. She snickered and remarked that I was a fool to commit to the Chapter 11 obligation at my age; I should have declared total bankruptcy like everybody else. I stood up and said: "Doesn't integrity, honesty, self respect mean anything?" Then made the comment: "Goddamn you, I'll be around to put you away," and left.

I still had my Stearman, 400 Commanche, and SR-9 Stinson. Through the years, a finance company—operated by Carl Matherly, a former World War II belly turret gunner on B-17s—in Des Moines, Iowa, provided me funds for my business.

Knowing that The Investor had his eye on my other airplanes, I sold all three to Carl for operating capital for my new company. He volunteered to hold them as long as necessary and would not sell them out from under me unless I requested. He kept his word. I did not fly them all those years. I couldn't afford to; the business came first. After thirteen years, I bought them back and flew the Stearman to Oshkosh '91.

With the funds for operating capital, I progressed reasonably well. On January 1st, 1978, I made my first payment of $1,000. Waiting for remittances, hiring more toolmakers, and purchasing materials, cash was tight. On February 1st, I called The Investor's attorney to tell him that I would be a few days late on the second payment. He was told to file a lawsuit against me for failure to make the payment on time. The attorney called me back with that information and wanted to know where the three airplanes were. I told him the truth. I had sold them for operating capital. Then he wanted to know where the Hawk was. That did it. I reminded him that the building more than satisfied my debt to The Investor; the $75,000 I had agreed to was to expedite confirmation of the plan.

It was a Friday Morning. I knew of an attorney who supposedly hated The Investor. I met with him before noon and instructed him to file a suit for breach of contract on the original agreement to provide the capital committed to for the expansion program. He was elated, said he'd always wanted to get this man. He would go after him and hang his scalp on a pole. The suit had to be filed that afternoon.

I left his office in a rage. I was trembling, could not control myself. There was no way in God's name The Investor would get his hands on the Hawk. I went to my office and tried to compose myself. It was 6:00 P.M., Friday afternoon. I was out of control. An employee had left a pistol with me. I took it out of my desk, got in my car and drove to The Investor's mansion. The steel gates were open. I drove up the circular drive to the door, got out of the car in a rage, trembling violently. I grabbed the pistol, walked to the front door, rang the bell and waited for him to come, my arm extended, the gun aimed at where his chest would be. The minutes passed. I waited, kept ringing the doorbell. No one came. I knew he answered his door most of the time. I stood there, it seemed forever; still no one. Shaking and unsteady, I started screaming for him to come out. I will never know how long I stood there. Finally, I heard footsteps. Too much time had passed. I was beginning to realize what I was doing. I nearly fell to the ground as I turned to jump in my car and leave before I committed murder.

I drove home, cursing the man who had destroyed 32 years of my life and now wanted to seize my lifelong dream and obsession. I stumbled into the house, crying violently. Angie grabbed me, sat me in a chair, hysterical, asked me what had happened. I tried to explain while she tried to hold me upright in the chair. Suddenly, I felt an explosion in my head, slipped out of her arms, and fell to the floor. She called an ambulance, which rushed me to the hospital.

The lawsuit I filed against The Investor was dismissed after twenty-two months. The attorney had not complied with a court order. He was supposed to have responded within a three week period, but had not. I filed a malpractice suit against him. The attorney handling it also malpracticed, and another attorney malpracticed on the suit against the second attorney.

The tortious lawsuit filed against the group that had taken all my toolmakers and medical business was also dismissed because two attorneys again had not complied with court orders. In all, I had seven attorneys malpractice on those two lawsuits. And I lost all possibility of recovering any part of my losses. It has been suggested that there were payoffs to some of the attorneys representing me in these lawsuits.

The new company was in operation four months. I could not be laid up too long, either in the hospital or at home. I had massive obligations to take care of and had to get back to the plant. My speech had not been affected too severely. By my choice, the stay in the hospital was short; I stayed home only a few days. I used crutches at home, had a wheelchair at the plant.

During the five years I had been operating in the previous large plant, I hired a young engineer right out of college. He learned quickly as a result of exposure to the practical side of tool and die design and production; he became my right hand man. I guided him through all phases of the business, including bidding and costing. He was extremely helpful during this difficult period.

From the time of confirmation, August 11, 1977, to December, 1982—5½ years—I built the company up to 32 employees, of which 18 were tool and die makers. During that period, I reduced the $3,000,000 obligation down to $55,000. The Investor had received $1,365,000 in the form of real estate and cash, which more than satisfied his claim. He was not satisfied. He attempted to take my home and was still after the Hawk.

Angie called me at work one day to let me know two men were outside surveying the house. I called The Investor's attorney and suggested that he instruct them to stay away in the future. He agreed, said he had no knowledge of this activity and would inform his client to drop any further attempt to acquire the home since his claim was satisfied. The Hawk was another matter; The Investor would not leave it alone.

From August of 1975—when I moved the Hawk out of the plant— right up to the time of confirmation of the plan of reorganization on August 11, 1977, The Investor had been trying to find the airplane. Shortly after I moved it to the airport, he found out it was in a T hangar. He owned a Lear jet and came to the airport frequently. One of the line boys innocently had mentioned that he'd seen the Hawk when I'd taken it to the airport. No one knew that I had moved it a short time later, after dark. I had special trailers for the fuselage and wings, so moving could be accomplished in minutes.

For the two-year period before confirmation of the plan of reorganization, two private detectives had been hired to follow me every time I left home. I never went near where the Hawk was stored. From August, 1975, to October, 1987, I moved the airplane ten times and as far as 225 miles from Omaha. The moves were always made in bad weather when no one was around; even the private eyes didn't venture out.

The most nerve-wracking move was during a snowstorm. The fuselage and wings were covered with bedsheets and plastic film on top to prevent them from getting wet. I planned to begin at 1:00 A.M. in the morning. When the first move was made out of the big building, several people helped. After that, only myself and my older brother moved the Hawk. It had started snowing late in the evening. I decided this was good cover. By the time we began the move, the snow was 2 to 3 inches deep, wind blowing 10 to 15 mph. The trip was about 20 miles, from one side of town to the other. The fuselage was not a problem; it was secure on the special trailer we had built. The top wing, mounted leading edge up in a horizontal plane was difficult to control. My brother drove the tow car as I stood on the trailer to control sway of the wing. It was a long, slow, nervous drive. That storage location was within a mile of The Investor's estate.

The second storage location turned into an unpleasant experience. One of my employees knew a farmer on the west side of Omaha who had an empty barn I could rent. A few months later, he came to the plant to see me. Unknown to any of us, this farmer knew The Investor. The farmer suggested that the rent on the barn should be increased substantially to better protect the Hawk. I told him I would think about it. Two days later, Sunday morning, when I knew he and his family would be gone for several hours, my brother and I hitched up the trailers and moved the Hawk out within minutes; his blackmail scheme did not work. Still not realizing that the airplane was gone, he called me a week later. I told him I refused his suggestion, and he could do whatever he wanted. I never heard from him again.

The longest move was the trip to Ottumwa, Iowa—225 miles. Jerry Strunk, standby pilot for the Hawk, operated Midwest Aviation at Ottumwa Industrial Airport. Jerry offend to work on the airplane if I would bring it to his facility. He remodeled a special work room for the Hawk. A short time later, he terminated his company, and we stored the airplane once again until I could bring it home.

CHAPTER EIGHTEEN
Subterfuge and Deceit

In the latter part of 1980, we began to build special packaging equipment for the pharmaceutical industry. I initiated the basic designs of the machinery then turned over the drawing and detailing to The Engineer and one of the draftsmen. The units were complicated and computer-controlled. We built a prototype machine, followed by orders for two more production units. These were expensive, $450,000 and more depending on how they were to be equipped.

The Engineer was becoming very knowledgeable in the design and function of the equipment. He had always appeared to be honest, loyal, dependable, and dedicated. I was 64 years old and hoped to retire so I could get the Hawk finished. I had reduced the Chapter 11 obligation to $55,000. I made an arrangement with the engineer to take over the company in the next year after I paid off the balance of debt. He seemed pleased with the offer; he was going to take over with practically no invested capital. Then in October of 1982 he began acting uneasy and withdrawn. I asked if he had personal problems. He said he had none. I was puzzled. We kept discussing arrangements of his takeover in the near future. He was agreeable to everything we planned, but was still acting strange.

December 27, 1982, another shock wave: I learned that The Engineer was having secret meetings with the former Chairman of the Board of the bank that had closed me down in September, 1975. He knew that I was doing well enough to retire the massive Chapter 11 debt. He had moved to Grand Rapids, Michigan, and set up a label manufacturing plant for his son. They would meet secretly with my Engineer either in Omaha or weekends at O'Hare Field in Chicago to discuss and make arrangements to set up a machine shop in west Omaha, take all my tool-makers and draftsman, and transfer building of the special machines to their new operation. They had told the pharmaceutical customer I was overcharging; they said they would do the work more cheaply.

Once again, mass exodus. I lost all my men—15 went with The Engineer, leaving one, my brother. They had offered the men wage increases and more overtime. There has never been loyalty among toolmakers. It is historic that they move from shop to shop making demands on the shop owners.

And another unbelievable situation. I went to the courthouse to learn who the incorporators of the new company were. Another surprise: the attorneys representing the creditors of my Chapter 11 repayment program had set up the corporation, precluding my ability to pay the $55,000 balance still due creditors. I set up a meeting to inform them that I could no longer continue payments. They were in a conflict of interest position in setting up a corporation that took all my people, but they still represented the creditors and the bankruptcy court. They suggested, and they would recommend to the bankruptcy court, that I sell the machinery to pay the balance of the debt. Then asked if I was going to sue them. I knew no attorney would sue one of their own kind. I had been through that before. Instead, I wrote a ten page letter to the bankruptcy judge explaining what had happened and that I could no longer make payments on the debt still owed. As a result, he gave me a complete release and discharged the case.

My next step was to file a tortious interference lawsuit against all parties and the new company that had taken my employees and business. Two attorneys were handling the case. They failed to comply in time with court orders, and the case was dismissed. I could do nothing about it; they canceled their charges to me and once again I lost. To try to find another attorney to sue them for malpractice in Omaha, as with the bankruptcy attorneys, would have been a waste of time. All this resulted in another delay to get the Hawk going.

It was 1983; I was 65 years old, knocked down again. Now what would I do? I had to get the Hawk finished somehow. I estimated that it would cost $150,000 to complete it. The only source of income would be to get the business going once again. I had lost the tool and die manpower, but still had the production and stamping operation. The income from that department could barely keep me afloat, so I had to find and hire toolmakers. In the next year I managed to bring the tool and die force up to four men, not enough to generate adequate income. In order to move faster, I needed more capital. During the period I was paying off the bankruptcy debt, I'd been able to acquire a Cessna 310R; I sold it and used the funds to speed building up the business. By 1985, the company was beginning to stabilize. I brought the Hawk home from Ottumwa, Iowa, planning to finish it in the next two years. But it was not to be. The ugly side of fate struck again, this time in the worst way. The unending pattern of my life.

CHAPTER NINETEEN

The Ultimate Tragedy:
The Loss of a Loved One

In early 1986, my wife Angie was diagnosed with cancer and required major surgery. The prognosis was not encouraging; she had maybe up to five years, but this was doubtful. It turned out to be four and a half years. I lost her February 16, 1991.

The last three and a half years, I devoted every day, every hour, I could to her. She was terminal; nothing else was important. The Hawk was completely forgotten. The business suffered; I relied on my employees. They did the best they could, I couldn't expect them to handle a struggling company. In Angie's last year I was with her twenty-four hours a day. While at the hospital, I slept in a chair by her bedside every single night of the many months that she was in a regular room. The many, many days and nights that she was in intensive care, I wasn't allowed into her room, so would sit in the hall outside the door and would sneak into the area and watch her through the window.

Angie was a tough little Italian gal. Her will to live was powerful. After massive surgery, she was in intensive care for about three weeks. The doctors told me that she would not recover. Then, in the middle of the night, a nurse came out in the hall and told me to go to Angie's room. I was amazed. She was sitting upright in bed, had pulled all the life support and oxygen tubes from her face, looked at me somewhat perturbed and exclaimed: *"Where have you been?"*

The stay in the hospital was four and a half months. Insurance benefits had expired after three months, the hospital was pressing me to take her home, but I refused. She was in no condition to be moved, so I agreed to self pay. By the first of December, 1990, the hospital was demanding that we leave. I would not put her in a nursing home. I prepared the family room at my home with a hospital bed and all the equipment to care for her.

Angie had been improving slowly in the hospital. When she got home, her improvement was phenomenal. I mixed all the IV medications and applied them. I cooked her meals. Everyone said she would never walk. With a therapist helping, she did with a walker—with difficulty, but she managed to walk.

During the week, we had a nurse's aid. On Saturday and Sunday, Angie wanted to be alone with me. I would pick her up off the bed, set her in a wheelchair, and we would drive around the house, so she could survey her home to make sure that I was taking care of it properly.

The bed was a regular hospital bed intended for one person. When Angie felt better, she asked if I would lie in the bed with her at night so she could sleep more easily. Well, I tried. She would scoot over to one side—the side rails up, padded with pillows—then I would try to lie sideways with the rails pressing against my back. It was really comical. She would lay her head on my shoulder, look me in the eyes, smile, give a soft sigh and say: "Now I can sleep. Thank you, Dear."

Towards the end, one day when I was tending to her needs, I bent down, kissed her, and said: "Honey, I don't think you know how much I really love you, more than you will ever know." She answered: "I know. Just for that, I'm going to live another year." Two days later we lost her. Everybody loved Angie. She was a basic, compassionate person. At our Catholic church, five priests participated in the funeral service, all of them her friends. I sang Schubert's "Ave Maria" and Angie's favorite song, "Come Back To Sorrento," in Italian. It took every bit of fortitude I had, but I had to do it. Then I almost collapsed. Then the *coup de grace*: without the courtesy of a notice, the hospital filed a lien against me for an erroneous bill in the amount of $232,000. I took care of that in a hurry by calling a meeting with the hospital president. They settled for much less.

CHAPTER TWENTY

In Limbo

The loss of a loved one is devastating beyond description. Everyone has their level of acceptance: mine is very low. First, the overwhelming pain, then the combination of anger and loss of faith. And the guilt. All the years we spent Saturday evenings and Sundays working on the Hawk, depriving my wife of vacations and the things normal people do. She never complained. If she couldn't help at certain times, she would read the paper or watch television in the workshop. Reflecting on all this, I came to hate the Hawk. There were times I felt like putting a match to it. For months I refused to go near it.

My obsession to have a P6-E had overpowered my logic and consideration for my loved ones. Additionally, the financial burden of building the Hawk affected our private life. It is difficult for an observer to comprehend the astronomical cost of building a real airplane. Although I had a large manufacturing facility, I paid for all materials and every hour of labor out of my pocket. I did not bury any of the charges in the company costs of operation.

A few weeks after I lost Angie, I tried to go back to work. Once again, the business was in shambles. My employees had not serviced customers properly, and they had gone elsewhere. During my absence, several toolmakers had left because the continued operation of the company was uncertain. I decided to try to sell it as a going business, had no luck. This left me with only one choice: build it up again.

Occasionally, I would go to the airport, take the Stearman out, and go flying. But my heart wasn't in it any more. As Oshkosh '91 approached, I had no thoughts of going. Terry Fritsch, who later would work on the Hawk, encouraged and virtually forced me to go. The morning I took off I almost turned around and came back.

I had to be in Omaha Friday the weekend of Oshkosh '91, so I went ten days before the start of activities. I hadn't flown much the previous year. When I arrived at Oshkosh, I made the worst three landings-in-one in my life. As I taxied up to the R&D hanger I felt like shrinking down in the cockpit (as I'd done when the CAA inspector had caught me flying underage in 1933). I hadn't expected a reception committee. Waiting to greet me were Paul Poberezny, Gene Chase, and several of the boys. I am sure they all saw my triple landing. Paul embraced me and gave me a warm welcome. It was great to see Gene Chase after all the years; we'd known each other a long time, back to the days of the beginning of the EAA and Antique Airplane Association. Tom Poberezny had graciously offered to store the Stearman in the R&D hangar while I was gone. When the convention started, Gene Chase taxied the Stearman to the parking area. I returned Saturday morning of the fly-in week end.

I had not been to an EAA annual fly-in since the last year at Rockford, Illinois, where my Stinson Gullwing SR-9 had been awarded Antique Grand Champion. I'd had the Stearman there also, restored in a highly customized configuration.

I was in awe of the new installation at Oshkosh; I describe it as an aviation Disney World. The variety and number of aircraft were unbelievable. The museum is outstanding. In my opinion, one of the best. I had not been to fly-ins or conventions for thirteen years because of all my problems. I renewed old friendships. Some were surprised to see me, assuming I had departed the good earth. Everyone was so accommodating, especially Gene Chase, who adopted me during my stay. And as I had expected they would, everyone asked about progress of the Hawk.

Strolling around the many display areas of the multitude of different types and designs of aircraft fueled my thoughts to get the Hawk project in motion. *All* these airplanes were beautiful and moreso in the eyes of those impassioned with a particular type, make, or design. Being from the old school—the Golden Age of Aviation—the antiques, classics, were my interest. And there was only one truly beautiful airplane— the Curtiss Hawk P6-E. And that opinion was shared by a majority of one—*me*.

I left Thursday morning, the last day of Oshkosh '91, taxied out to the runway, and ground-checked the engine before take-off. When ready, I looked to the flagman for wave-off. He walked towards me, reached up to give me a farewell handshake. It was Buck Hilbert, that old goat who had been the ring leader years ago, the last EAA fly-in at Rockford, who had been unhappy with my highly modified Stearman. Some years later he stopped in Omaha to see the Hawk progress and gleefully informed me that he was the bad guy who criticized my airplane, called it a circus wagon—thereafter I called him an old goat. The flight home that day was beautiful, sunshine all the way, the air smooth as glass. I had plenty time to think about the Hawk.

CHAPTER TWENTY-ONE
Rebirth of A Hawk

The first thing I did when I got back from Oshkosh '91 was go to the shop building where I had stored the Hawk. I got a chair, sat down, stared at it, and began to reflect about what to do. I loved the airplane—and I hated it. Should I finish it—or put a match to it. This monster had changed the course of thirty years of my life. To provide the funds to complete it would be a problem. My earlier estimate to finish it was approximately $150,000, which proved to be low. I had no available cash. I had to build the business up one more time, but that would take too long to generate enough in the form of wages to me. As I stated earlier, I paid for construction of the Hawk from my personal funds. The few people close to the project and my circumstances suggested I take a partner. But no way on God's earth would I do that after all these years.

There was a solution, however. It meant more personal sacrifice, but I guess very few people would consider what I did a sacrifice. When you struggle all your life to acquire material things that become very dear to you and give them up after years of adversity, maybe that is sacrifice. I had my Stearman, Stinson, 400 Commanche, and a North American AT-6A (unrestored). The Stearman and Stinson are part of me; I will never part with them. The Commanche meant just as much, but if I decided to finish the Hawk, I had to sell something. It was the Commanche. That would provide initial funds to get the project going. Next, the AT-6A went, and it was a beautiful polished airplane.

When both left Omaha, I am not ashamed to admit that I broke down and cried. All for that damned Hawk. If this seems strange to you who are reading this, re-read my story before you judge me. And the sale of those two airplanes *still* was not enough. When the funds were used up, I borrowed another $50,000 from my friend in Des Moines, Iowa, who stuck with me through the years. Not once did he refuse me help when I needed it. Carl Matherly, the World War II belly turret gunner on B-17s who was shot down twice, crashed, but survived. Perhaps destiny had determined that he was to share in development of the Hawk. I could not have built it without his financial aid. Through the years, he had provided me funds to build the Hawk as well as for my business ventures.

Having made the decision to finish the Hawk, I had to concentrate on business as well as handle procuring items for the airplane, but I could only work on it in what little spare time I had. The finest automobile restoration man I knew, Terry Fritsch, had worked for me on classic cars I'd owned at one time. When I'd brought the Stearman and Commanche home, he'd done a beautiful job of reconditioning them. He was the right man for the Hawk. Terry is a race car and drag racer and was national champion at one time. Gene Stanley, one of my top toolmakers, is a sky diver, hand glider flier, artist, and internationally-known mountain climber. These two would work on the airplane. My retired younger brother, a top toolmaker, would do all the machine work and make many parts still needed. To complete the Hawk P6-E crew and staff, I needed a public relations manager and administrator to handle publicity and promotional planning; this would be Russ DeVoe, past commander of the Great Plains branch of the Confederate Air Force and present vice president of the Omaha EAA Chapter 80. Standby pilot for the Hawk is Jerry Strunk of Ottumwa, Iowa, a corporate pilot. Our ground crew member is Art Hill—one of my past employees—who helped me with moving and working on airplanes many times through the years. With the staff completed, we held many meetings to set up schedules and promotional activities. With the funds available to proceed, Terry and Gene began work in early December 1991, completion set for no later than May 1st of 1992. We had committed for first public showing of the Hawk to coincide with the regional EAA fly-in scheduled for June 7th. This plan slowly went down the drain as problems developed, not only with the structure, but also—and more critically—with the Curtiss Conqueror engine that was supposed to be ready to run.

Looking at the Hawk before we started to work on it, one would assume it was ready for final paint scheme. Throughout the ten moves in the past fifteen years, I had not damaged or even scratched the airplane. There had been some deterioration after having been stored all those years in hot, cold, and damp locations. The project turned into a major restoration of a new airplane.

Dick Cooper of Atchison, Kansas, well-known for his paint brush technique of painting airplanes, offered to refinish the tail feathers and ailerons to help expedite the project. I loaded these parts in a trailer and delivered them to him. He did a beautiful job.

The wings were finished in final color; I hand-painted the stars and letters using Dick Cooper's paint brush method, but some cosmetic work was still needed around the N and cabane strut fittings. Cynthia Almquist, a specialist in fabric work from Brown's Airport, Inc. at Weeping Water, Nebraska, took care of that. Her partner, George Schworm—an ex World War pilot—later helped us with advice and guidance, rigged the airplane, and at the end helped us with the engine.

We removed all sheet metal from the fuselage and stripped it bare. Hoses, fuel and oil lines removed from the engine. The tubing framework and engine mount were sanded and repainted with Durathane in the correct color.

All engine cowling sheet metal, having been hand-formed, needed final finishing. The radiator cowling, a masterpiece of workmanship by Herb Tischler, required minor cosmetics. The wheel pants were not finished, but we completed the lamination strips and attach fittings to mount them solidly to the framework on the landing gear.

None of the lower wing root streamline fairings had been made when the project had been stopped years before. To shape and fit them properly required that the bottom wings be attached to the fuselage. We accomplished this by stringing a cable from a cabane strut fuselage fitting to an outer N strut wing bracket. The cable had a turnbuckle attached to adjust to the proper dihedral. Terry and Gene did a nice job hand-forming and fitting these parts.

The upper landing gear cuff fairings were the most difficult to finish. Herb had them partially done when he'd left, but they were not final-fitted nor was the edge closing arrangement completed. I made drawings off the factory blueprints and paper patterns for Terry and Gene to work from. To fit these cuffs properly, the airplane had to be both in ground and in flight condition. The cuffs are hinged and attached at the top to the side of the fuselage. The landing gear struts slide up and down inside the cuffs during taxiing, take-off, and landing. We hooked a come-along binder to the tow lugs on the axles, put slide cloths under the tires, and drew the gear together to flight condition. In this position, the cuffs close alongside the radiator cowling to seal the gap.

The thin plywood wing walks were blanked out, and Gene mounted them to the top of the lower wings then glued on the cork facing. To insure that they will not peel off, there is a close pattern of brass screws along the edges. Gene did a neat cosmetic job, but he had to do it over again a short time later because the glue did not hold, and the cork bubbled. To protect the pretty cork finish, Terry made strap-on covers to use during engine and taxi runs.

We decided to paint the fuselage and all metal parts with Durathane. We found it to be tough and almost scratch-proof. The wings and tail feathers are dope. I did not intend for the finish to be so shiny; it almost looks hand-rubbed. The spray job was so good that the dope flowed out smoothly. All fasteners were left natural except where they fell within the Hawk paint scheme. The cockpit is painted silver.

With the painting behind us, the next step was the engine compartment. We removed the radiator and took it to be pressure checked in order to make sure that there were no leaks. The water pump packing was inspected for ageing, metal coolant lines removed and reinstalled with new gaskets. The rubber coolant hoses installed by the engine rebuild shop were incorrect and could have ruptured; we had to replace them with high-temperature hose; that cost $3 per inch.

Getting into the functional parts of the engine, we installed all new sparkplugs, removed the overhead valve covers, and checked valve clearances. While the sparkplugs were out, we checked the condition of the inside of the cylinders. They all were shiny, no rust. The engine rebuilder had prepared the engine well for storage. We pressure-oiled the engine before attempting to rotate it. We were pleased and relieved that it turned freely. We assumed that the magnetos, distributors, fuel pump, oil pump, and two huge carburetors were OK and that they had been rebuilt by the engine rebuilder.

The last thing we did before moving to the airport was paint the Snow Owl on both sides of the fuselage and the number 60 on the nose. For years I had been trying to find a clear, detailed picture of the bird. There are many pictures of it in magazines and other publications, but none are clear enough. Time was running out; I had to decide on one. I have a good side view of P6-E #74. I projected the picture full size and traced it, adding detail as best I could from the picture. Terry and I spent hours and hours in libraries looking at pictures of Snow Owls, but we could not find one with the right attack posture. I had to use the picture on airplane #74. The artist and I worked together, trying to decide the detail, as he painted the bird on the airplane. He finished it, and, considering what he'd had to work with, he did an excellent job. We knew that the profile was correct; it hadn't been a problem to trace the blow-up. It was the feather detail we could not determine.

Then, the *same day* that the artist finished, I received a package that had a clear picture of the Snow Owl with excellent feather detail. Now I was in a real quandary, but there was only one decision I could make: sand the bird off the airplane and paint the new one on. Terry tried to discourage me, but I got fine sand paper and solvent and went to work removing the painting. What a mess. The artist was not particularly enthusiastic about doing it again. But he did. And it came out great and correct.

CHAPTER TWENTY-TWO
More Ground Time

It was time to move. For the first time in 32 years, the Hawk would finally come to roost in one piece at an airport. Don Smithey, manager of Omaha Eppley Airfield, made available the airport equipment storage hangar for assembly of the Hawk. Don and all the airport personnel went out of their way to accommodate us, providing the privacy we needed; we had the freedom to come and go in a secured area at all hours of the day or night.

We loaded the fuselage on its special trailer, hopefully for the last time. To avoid heavy traffic, we left late in the evening and arrived at the airport before dark. We were greeted by a group of security guards in case we needed help. Early the next morning we loaded the top wing on its special trailer. The 32-foot wing swayed easily, I picked the shortest route. It was a Saturday morning. As we neared the airport, we found that the streets were blocked off for runners, and—even though there was plenty of room to drive to one side of them—the police would not let us through. The officer was abusive and forced me to turn around and drive eight miles farther around a lake to get back to approximately the same spot he'd made us leave. A breeze was starting to blow, and it was a nervous drive. Two more loads, and everything was at the hangar. We were ready to start assembly of the Hawk.

The first phase was to mount the top wing. We built two wooden horses to the height of the bottom of the wing in level flight. We attached a block-and-tackle to a hangar roof beam, bolted a sling to the lift brackets on top of the wing, then hoisted the wing high enough to place the horses under the wing tips, one at each end. We rolled the fuselage under the center of the wing at the location where the cabane struts fit, lifted the tail to flying level—set on a special tripod—and attached the cabane struts and wires. It now became a parasol, and we removed the horses and hoist.

Next, we attached the bottom wings under the guidance and supervision of Debbie Bonacci, wife of Don, operators of the North Omaha Airport. Her knowledgeable flow of instructions kept Terry and Gene on their toes, and her skillful support of the wings at the tips was unequalled. Then the N struts and flying and landing wires went on, completing wing assembly. After the tail feathers were mounted, George Schworm from Brown's Airport, Inc. at Weeping Water, Nebraska, rigged the airplane and performed the weight and balance.

It was time to add seven and a half gallons of oil and eight gallons of pure ethylene glycol to the engine. The airplane had to be in flight level position to fill the system. Absolutely no water was to be added; that could create steam as the engine temperature rose. As stated previously, pressure buildup could cause the surge tank to expand and possibly explode. This did in fact happen to Colonel Paul Jacobs, the engineering officer at Selfridge Field, in P6-E #56, in October of 1933. His goggles and windshield were covered with hot Glycol, and he had to make a forced landing.

June 7, 1992, was set for the first public showing and flight of the Hawk. It was the 6th of June; we had only one day left. We'd worked frantically to prepare the airplane. Other than a few items yet to be made, the airplane was ready to fly. Or should have been.

As the airplane was towed out to the ramp for the first start-up of the engine, I sat in the cockpit to get a feel for the brakes. At the instructions of Don Smithey, the airport manager, several fire trucks were on hand to protect me and the airplane in case of fire. Don was enthralled with the Hawk and made sure every safety precaution was implemented

The capacities of the main gas tank in front of the pilot and the belly drop tank are each fifty gallons. We put only thirty gallons in the main tank for the initial start. As in the original airplanes, there is a hand-operated wobble pump to build fuel pressure; the engines did not have electric pumps.

The wheel chocks were in place. I set the brakes and began stroking the wobble pump, kept stroking the wobble pump it seemed forever. It is located at the bottom of the gas tank, a long distance to the top of the engine. The two huge carburetors are mounted on top of a massive intake manifold nestled in between the cylinder banks. I was beginning to wonder if thirty gallons of fuel in the main gas tank was enough to fill the carburetors and intake manifold. Finally, the fuel gage showed signs of pressure. I then gave six pumps of the primer, per the engine manual, energized the electric inertia starter to high pitch, engaged it to turn the engine a few revolutions to fuel the cylinders. I repeated the procedure a second time, turned the magneto switch on, and jerked the impulse coil that is attached to the starter engage cable.

The engine coughed and died. This went on for hours during which we removed all cowling, checked carburetor settings, linkage, fuel supply, everything we could think of. George Schworm—an engine specialist—Terry, Jerry Strunk, and Gene all could not arrive at any conclusions. It was approaching dusk, so we towed the Hawk back to the hangar and sat for hours into the night reviewing several engine manuals; we have an original factory manual and many subsequent ones describing modifications and improvements through the years.

The Hawk was supposed to be at the Sky Harbor hangar by 10:00 A.M. Sunday. We knew that the airplane would not fly that day. I insisted we try to get it running enough to a least taxi across the field and make a respectable appearance, but no one agreed. It was 8:00 A.M.; we had two hours left. I tried time after time to get it to run. No luck. The engine would cough, sputter, and die as though it were not getting enough gas. I finally got it running by aggressively stroking the wobble pump as it fired, kept working it as I increased the RPM, and let the engine-driven fuel pump take over. Even then, I had to work the hand pump to keep the engine running; this indicated a weak fuel pump. But pumping excessive gas into the carburetors and engine resulted in a near catastrophe. As the engine fired, a huge ball of fire erupted from the right cylinder bank, inches below the top wing. Fireman jumped up and ran to the trucks. Terry and Gene grabbed fire extinguishers and rushed to the plane. I felt a flash of heat on the right side of the cockpit. A cloud of black smoke and hot oil poured out of the left bank, I ducked behind the windshield, but some oil hit the side of my face. The engine cleaned out and was running, but not well. I signaled that I was going to taxi across the field. At the halfway point, another problem developed; the glycol temperature began to increase slowly, then climbed just below maximum allowable. I had to shut the engine down, and the airplane had to be towed the rest of the way.

As I sat in the cockpit during the trip across the airport I became angry at the engine rebuilder. The engine was supposed to have been completely rebuilt, all accessories brought back to new factory specifications. They had the engine overhaul and rebuild manuals; there was no excuse for what was happening. And I can say that unequivocally after what we discovered progressively the next several months.

In spite of all these problems, Sunday June 7, 1992, was a good day. Hundreds attended, many EAA members in for the regional gathering—Tom Poberezny, Bob Mackey, Jim Koepnick (from EAA Headquarters in Oshkosh), and Bob Taylor (president of the Antique Airplane Association). Omaha's Mayor P. J. Morgan proclaimed this date as Hawk P6-E day.

At the close of the program, I again insisted on trying to start the engine and taxi away into the sunset. Terry tried to discourage me, but I just couldn't disappoint all these people who had been kind enough to attend the showing. I tried time and time again. Terry insisted I give up, but I refused, kept trying, a little gentler with the wobble pump. The engine started, fortunately no fireball this time. I slowly drove off into the sunset, gently stroking the wobble pump, the engine struggling to run, and made it to the shop hangar. The glycol was at maximum temperature, so we had to drain it immediately. If overheated, it becomes highly caustic and can cause damage to the inside of the engine.

CHAPTER TWENTY-THREE
An Exercise in Futility

June 7th to late July, six weeks, seemed plenty of time to get all the engine problems resolved, fly off the required 25 hours, and still make it to Oshkosh '92. It was not to be. By mid-November, we finally got the engine running nicely, but other problems developed.

The first item we took off the engine was the fuel pump. We set it up on a test stand to check fuel flow pressure and volume; it was nowhere near enough to supply the carburetors. The pump was completely worn out, the gears and shafts beyond repair, bushings worn egg-shaped and scored. I had a spare pump, but it, too, was worn beyond use. If I could not find a good one, we would have to make new gears, rebush the housing, and machine the pump body to remove wear grooves.

Terry and I called all over the country for three days trying to find a pump. A specialty repair shop in California had a vane type with the correct mounting base and drive that could produce much more pressure and the flow we needed. We mounted it, started the engine, and this solved the pump problem.

The engine was running rich, kicking out clouds of black smoke from the rear six cylinders, but snapping and spitting from the front half as though it were lean. To expedite checking and possibly rebuilding the carburetors, I decided to take them to a specialty shop in Tulsa, Oklahoma, that had been recommended.

We took along a spare to inspect before we opened up the ones off the Hawk, after which the top was removed from the rear carburetor, the one that seemed to be flooding most of the time. Then came the first surprise: there was no gasket between the top and bottom. Silicon had been used. Gas had dissolved it between the bowel chambers, causing overflow into the manifold and flooding the engine. Next, the metering pin and seat were worn and deeply grooved, preventing them from shutting off the gas supply. The butterflies were not set together, one of them open approximately one sixteenth of an inch when the throttle was closed.

It had been a wise decision to go to the specialty shop. They had the tools and equipment to rework the jets and furnish new metering pins. New gaskets were made, float level set, and the rear carburetor was assembled. Terry and I flew back to Omaha and continued working on the engine until the second one was finished and shipped to us.

Next, we checked the dual magneto. The first thing we found wrong was another surprise. The manual states the magneto can be set permanently in the full advance position and has an automatic retard arrangement when the engine is started. To our amazement, the magneto was permanently fixed in the *full retard* setting of fifteen degrees, and timing to the engine was off another twenty, making a total of thirty-five degrees in an extreme retarded position. And the clearance of one set of points was locked open, burned, pitted, and not functioning. It is a wonder that the engine ran at all. We had to make special adapters to mount the magneto on a test machine to check it, the coil, and the condenser. George Czarnicki of Central Cylinder Engine Rebuilders in Omaha was most accomodating in allowing us to use his shop test equipment and helping us correct all the problems we discovered.

While mounting the magneto, we noticed oil dripping from the ends of the two distributor drive shafts. There is an oil hole on top of the back cover plate to lubricate them. The shafts have a rotary spiral groove to carry the excess oil away from the rotors and contact points in the distributor cap. We removed them to inspect the shafts and the bushings. More surprises. They were badly worn, had grooves in them—the bronze bushings egg-shaped—and the fit so sloppy that the oil (instead of expelling to the back of the distributors) was going forward into the caps and shorting sparks intermittently. We ground the diameter of the shafts and made new bushings to correct that problem.

We removed and inspected the oil pump, water pump, wobble pump, Cuno filter, sump pump, and every item that would come off the engine. There was no major problem with any of these parts. We had the second carburetor back and assumed that all we had to do was install both of them on the engine, and it would be ready to run. That thought turned into a month-long puzzle.

Mounting both carburetors to the huge intake manifold and installing the assembly between the cylinder banks was a project in itself. The block-and-tackle was still attached overhead, since we had mounted the top wing to the fuselage, and we used it to hoist the unit above the engine and lower it into position. All our apprehensions were behind us; we now knew that the engine had to function properly. Uh-huh.

We called the fire squad, towed the Hawk out to the ramp. I got in the cockpit and was careful not to over-prime the engine; the new powerful fuel pump would take over after a few revolutions. The engine did not fire on the first attempt. It snorted and stopped on the second. On the third, it took hold, but a ball of fire came from the right bank and clouds of black smoke from the left rear cylinders, just as before all the repairs we had made.

Terry was standing at the wing tip, shaking his head. I threw my arms up and let them hang over the side of the cockpit in total exasperation, climbed out of the airplane, dismissed the fire squad, and suggested to Terry that we go in the office and attempt to analyze this whole situation.

The next two days we sat and talked, walked in circles, sat and talked. Terry stated emphatically that he believed it still had to be a problem with the carburetors. We agreed, however, that this should not be; they had just been completely rebuilt. We again removed the complete unit from the engine and set it up on the test stand to check the floats and metering pins fuel flow holding pressures and found them to be correct. Next, we removed the covers, or top half of the carburetors, to check the float levels and repeated the pressure test to observe them in the open condition. They still checked OK and were holding at twice the required pressure. The only discrepancy we found was that the float in the front carburetor was too low, so we brought it up to the proper level of one quarter inch. The rear one was set properly. We removed the metering pins and seats; they mated perfectly, which was confirmed by the excessive pressure they held. For two days we repeated the tests with the same good results. We decided to mount the unit back on the Hawk and try again.

Once again, clouds of black smoke and fire poured out of the engine. This was maddening. Off came the carburetors. Back to the test equipment, again checked out good. We went back to the shop hangar, set the monster on the bench. Both of us sat staring at it. Terry had an idea. He removed the rear carburetor from the intake manifold and went back to the engine shop to try the thought he had. I stayed at the hangar to do my own thinking. I decided to remove the top of the front carburetor. There are two floats, each in its own chamber, connected by a U-shaped clevis hinged at each side. The new gaskets were on the bottom half, hooked on the studs that held it together. The floats were resting on the bottom of the chambers. I lifted them up to see if they were free to move without interference or possibly sticking at the hinge pins. And what a shock! The gasket was overlapping the float chamber and preventing the float from rising to proper level and closing off the metering pin, causing the intake manifold to be flooded with gas.

I grabbed the carburetor, rushed to the engine shop, and showed Terry the problem. We immediately opened the other one and found the same condition. We were at a loss for words for a period of time. George, the shop owner, couldn't believe what he saw and—like us—stood shaking his head for a long time. We trimmed the gaskets and assembled the carburetors. *Now* we assumed that the problem was completely solved. Guess again. We hurried to the hangar, re-installed the carburetor assembly to the engine, and towed the Hawk out to the ramp. I jumped into the cockpit, elated and full of confidence that we would soon take wing. The big Conqueror coughed on the first try, took hold on the second, belched black smoke again, but no fire. The engine did keep running rough, kicking out puffs of black smoke, but not as badly as all the previous times. There was improvement. Terry dropped to his knees in total disgust, his head bowed, so I presumed that he was either praying or expressing himself some other way. I wasn't praying. There is one thing for certain: if I *ever* build another airplane, you can bet it will have a round engine, as in a Curtiss Hawk XF11C-2.

What do we do now? Take the carburetors off and go through them again? We did. And spent two days at the engine shop test equipment repeating everything we had done a dozen times, checked them with the tops on and off, float levels, made sure there were no more restrictions. I was sitting at the bench, staring at the front carburetor sitting right in front of me. I noticed something I had not seen before. One of the floats had a shiny spot on the top edge of it. Why should that be? All the floats were dull brass. I picked up the top half, or cover. Must I say how often I keep getting surprises, if not shocks? Happened again. The cover had a chafe mark above where the float shiny spot was. When the carburetor had been built at the factory, they'd not cast the cover deep enough; this resulted in the float striking the cover and stopping before the metering pin was seated, allowing gas to pass and flood the intake manifold and engine. More head-shaking. We carbide-ground the dome of the casting approximately one sixteenth of an inch deeper and solved that problem.

Every time we had tried to run the engine, it appeared that the rear carburetor was flooding because the clouds of black smoke were coming from the back cylinders. It actually had been the front carburetor causing the problem; it would not shut off—because of the float interference—and flood the huge intake manifold. The airplane sitting in the tail-down position, allowed the gas to flow to the back of the manifold and feed the excess fuel to the rear part of the engine, causing the flooding and clouds of black smoke. Terry and I were now convinced that we had solved all the problems. Don't give a sigh of relief; there is more to come.

Once again, call the fire trucks, tow the Hawk out to the ramp, and surprisingly, that big old engine fired the first hit, spun into life, and acted as if it was going to keep running—except for a new problem. One of the cylinders on the right front bank was snapping, spitting, and not firing. We shut the engine down, removed the right valve cover, thinking that it might be a stuck valve or improper clearance. It wasn't. Terry determined that it must be an electrical problem. We traced out the entire system and found a broken sparkplug wire encased in the two-foot long aluminum sheath that contains all the wires from the distributor to the engine. We replaced the wire. Once again the engine started on the first try and ran smoothly, purred like a kitten. Terry began walking in circles, both arms in the air, thumbs up, a big smile on his face. We had conquered the Conqueror. Almost—

Now I could finally run the engine to check its behavior and operating conditions. Oil temperature and pressure was normal at various RPM. Fuel pressure was stable. The Glycol temperature gage was indicating higher than normal range, but never went beyond maximum allowable. I was not comfortable with this. I removed the gage and took it to an instrument shop to be calibrated. It checked twenty degrees high, which meant that the coolant was not exceeding normal operating temperature. One last function that was not correct was the coolant system surge tank relief valve. During one run up of the engine, it did not release, pressure built up in the tank and caused it to bulge. As I stated before, the system operates at no pressure; buildup can be caused only if water is in the engine. We initially filled the system with propolyne glycol, which is less caustic and will not damage the inside of the engine if it deteriorates, as will pure ethelyn glycol. We were not informed that propolyne glycol contained ten percent water—which is prohibited in the Conqueror because it will generate stream and could explode the surge tank. The purpose of a relief valve is to prevent this. We had to fill the engine with pure glycol, run and flush it three times to clear out the propolyne mixture to make sure that all water was eliminated. But a relief valve is necessary. We replaced it three times before we found one sensitive enough to release at one pound of pressure. The gage to monitor this must be watched more frequently than any other engine function gage.

Terry and I were now satisfied that the engine was flyable. I began taxi tests, to get the feel of ground control, and was surprised at how sensitive the airplane was to the slightest rudder movement. After slow and fast runs on the ramps, I was comfortable with the way it handled. I was having trouble with the original automotivetype brakes operating smoothly or holding when I needed them. We reworked them several times without improvement. After what happened in the next week, I had to make the decision to change the brake system.

By the middle of October, 1992, the Hawk was ready to fly. We couldn't wait any longer; the weather was turning cold. The engine was operating nicely, and I had a good feel for ground control, so early on a Sunday morning we prepared for the first speed run down a runway. The temperature was 40 degrees; it took a little time to warm the engine. I taxied to the run-up pad at the end of the runway and performed a final check as outlined in the manual. The procedure calls for running the engine at wide open throttle for two minutes. I was standing on the brakes, but they would not hold over 1600 RPM, which was not enough for my purpose. The airplane was creeping, causing the shoes to rotate forward and lock up in the drums, and they would not release after I took my feet off the brake pedals. I increased the engine RPM and flipped the rudder and elevators to try to break them loose. They were locked solid. I had to shut down the engine and wait to be towed back to the hangar. This happened several times. Before we could try again, the weather turned bad, cold, and we had never ending snow. We were done for the winter.

I was extremely frustrated with the brake problem. Everything on the airplane was 100% original per factory blueprints; I couldn't accept the idea of installing modern brakes. When Terry and I visited Colonel Jacobs—the engineering officer at Selfridge Field during the thirties—in December of 1992, we asked him if they'd had problems with brakes on P6-Es. He had flown several of them; his was #56. They'd always flown off dirt fields. When the engines were just warm enough to fly, they would take off and seldom used brakes anytime.

It was a tough decision to make, but I felt that there was no choice. I envisioned myself in the Hawk, approaching the end of a runway, ready to touch down, and having to use the brakes for some reason or other. The mental picture of the airplane on its back or a wing torn off as a result of a ground loop, because a brake had locked, convinced me that I must modernize them. I decided to use Cleveland disc brakes. It was a major conversion, but was completed by the end of March, 1993.

During the month of April, I re-inspected the entire airplane to satisfy myself that it was ready for flight. The only items not complete were the eight "N" struts streamline fairings. There was one annoying condition: when the airplane sat for several days, oil would seep down from the oil tank through the sump pump gears and accumulate in the bottom at the rear cylinders and splatter the airplane with oil, requiring a couple hours of clean-up. I solved this problem by installing an oil sump quick drain valve. While the airplane is setting idle, a drain hose is slipped over the quick drain valve fitting, fed into a sealed five gallon drain bucket, and left on. Before an engine start, the valve is shut off, and the drained oil poured back into the oil tank. This way the airplane stays clean.

As of May 1, 1993, the Hawk was ready for taxiing to test the new brakes and ground handling. After sitting all winter, the engine fired on the first hit and ran beautifully. The new brakes were soft and effective. The sump drain worked as I had hoped; there was no discharge of oil from the rear cylinders, no clean-up necessary. After runway test runs, the Hawk was ready for first flight, which I hoped would be by mid-May, 1993.

CHAPTER TWENTY-FOUR
One for the Historians

On December 14, 1992, I met with 89-year-old Colonel Paul Jacobs, U.S. Air Force, Ret. He had been with the 17th Pursuit Squadron (they'd had the P6-E airplanes), and had been assigned to Selfridge Field, Michigan, after graduating from Kelly Field, Texas, in 1928; he'd flown various models of the Hawk before the P6-E. He'd been the engineering officer and flight leader at Selfridge Field, and had flown P6-E #32-256.

Practically all the problems we encountered in my airplane with the Curtiss Conqueror engine had been experienced back in 1931 and through the years the P6-E airplanes were in service. It had been Colonel Jacobs' responsibility to solve these problems.

Colonel Jacobs told us—myself and Terry Fritsch, who had accompanied me on the trip—things that contradict some of the stories I've heard and read through the years about Curtiss Hawk P6-E airplanes. The Colonel had dozens of original photographs he had taken during the period of the P6-Es, many at Selfridge Field.

According to Colonel Jacobs, the 17th Pursuit Squadron received several P6-Es in December, 1931. We saw a picture (dated December, 1931) of the line-up of these first airplanes. This may not contradict any historical information, but what we saw in the picture certainly does.

The story has always been that the P6-Es were painted in the gaudy paint scheme for the Cleveland Air Races in August of 1932. The Colonel stated emphatically that this was not so; the airplanes assigned to the 17th Pursuit Squadron were painted in that famous pattern as they were received at Selfridge Field. This was confirmed by the photograph taken in December of 1931.

Another point in question is the design of the Snow Owl painted on the sides of the P6-E fuselage. When I was trying desperately to find a clear picture of the bird for my P6-E, most of the historians had the same concept as mine—with the exception of one, Ken Wilson. He sent me a print of airplane #32-256 with a different version of the Snow Owl, along with a note betting me $1,000 that it was correct—not knowing that it was Colonel Jacobs' personal airplane. Now for the facts about that bird, according the Colonel.

The version of the Snow Owl painted on the P6-Es of the 17th Pursuit Squadron up to 1933 was used as far back as World War I. The one exception was the Squadron Commander, Hoyt, who had his own design of the bird. Colonel Jacobs was not satisfied with the posture of the Owl, so he went to Wright Field and had them redesign the bird to his liking. And that is the version of the bird—the one in the picture Ken Wilson sent me—that was eventually painted on all P6-Es after the gaudy paint scheme was replaced with different patterns. The Snow Owl I had painted on my P6-E is correct. I have original photographs of airplane #32-260, my serial number, showing the bird as I have it.

Almost every airplane buff has seen the picture of a line-up of P6-Es that flew at the Cleveland Air races in 1932. I had heard the story, many times, that one of the planes near the center slipped out of place, struck one next to it, and three airplanes crashed. Then, the next weekend, the same thing happened, and two more were lost. When I told Colonel Jacobs of this story, he said that it was absolutely not true; neither of the incidents had happened. He had been in the line-up, third from the far end. During the Air Show, when not participating in formation flying, he was flight testing a P6-E that had engine trouble and had to make a forced landing in a nearby field. He had not seen a ditch ahead, the wheels fell into it, and the airplane rolled "up in a ball," as the Colonel described it. He was not injured.

Before we concluded the meeting with Colonel Jacobs, I asked him about the reliability of the Curtiss Conqueror engine and the flying characteristics of the Curtiss Hawk P6-E. He said that after making all the modifications to the engine, he liked it very much and had complete confidence in it. And he considered the P6-E the most pleasant and enjoyable airplane he had ever flown; it had no bad habits. He was certainly qualified to make this determination because he had flown practically every type of fighter plane, and the first jets, before retiring in 1956.

The various buildings in which my tool and die company was located over the years (next six pages).

First location, 1948.

Second location, 1951.

Third location, 1953.

Fourth location, 1965.

Fifth location, the big building that I lost, 1969. My Flagship Building

Sixth and last location, 1977.

Scramble ! ! !
Me (?) at 75 (?????)